QUIZ WHIZ 2

1,000 SUPER FUN MIND-BENDING TOTALLY AWESOME TRIVIA QUESTIONS

NATIONAL GEOGRAPHIC

WASHINGTON, D.C.

Table of CONTENTS

6 Introduction

8 Animal Kingdom

The Wild Life	10
Catching Some ZZZs	12
Hi, Honey, I'm Home!	14
And Now for My Next Trick...	16
What's for Dinner?	18
Map Mania! Pals in Peril	20
Egg-cellent Animals	22
Going Ape	24
What's a Body to Do?	26
Home Sweet Home	28
Ultimate Animal Challenge	30

52 Pop Culture

Kid TV	54
Famous Villains	56
Movie Mania!	58
Starstruck	60
For Gamers Only!	62
Ultimate Pop Culture Challenge	64

 32 What on Earth?

Coast to Coast	34
Mark Your Calendar	36
Be a Good Sport!	38
On Location	40
Let's Talk Tradition!	42
Take Me to Your Leader	44
A Capital Idea!	46
Map Mania! Great Adventure	48
Ultimate Earthly Challenge	50

66 Get Back to Nature

Survival Guide	68
It's a Cookout!	70
A Starry Show	72
Map Mania! Wild Weather	74
Amazing Antarctica	76
Out at Sea	78
A Distinct Desert	80
Ultimate Nature Challenge	82

84 Blast from the Past

Flashback!	86
In Knightly Fashion	88
Rock On!	90
National Parks Road Trip!	92
Eat, Drink, and be Merry!	94
DragonVille	96
Famous Fiction	98
Animals Tamed by Time	100
Map Mania! World Travelers	102
Ultimate Blast from the Past Challenge	104

122 Weird Science

Body Parts	124
Creepy Creatures of the Deep	126
Text Me … LOL	128
Bugging Out	130
Out of This World	132
Test Your Eco-Smarts	134
Amazing Plants	136
Map Mania! Fantastic Fossil Finds	138
Ultimate Science Challenge	140

106 It All Adds Up!

Count Your Critters	108
Treasure Chest	110
And a One, and a Two, and a …	112
Know Your Numbers!	114
Trivia Tech Zone	116
Map Mania! Nations by the Numbers	118
Ultimate Number Challenge	120

142 Global Adventures

Only in America	144
Olympics Around the World	146
Rolling on the River	148
Cool Facts About China	150
Traveling Circus	152
Map Mania! Scuba Sights	154
Ultimate Global Challenge	156

158 Answers

171 Credits

INTRODUCTION

So you think you are tops with trivia? Get ready to test yourself as you blaze through 1,000 fascinating and funny questions. Strap on your thinking cap—and fasten your funny bone. *Quiz Whiz 2* is a high-energy, page-turning adventure that will take you around the world to learn about things as tiny as sesame seeds and places as big as China. You'll learn about some pretty incredible people, too—brave knights and explorers, superior athletes and Olympians, famous superstars and singers, and even a few wacky inventors!

Quiz Whiz 2 has pages and pages of silly, serious, and spellbinding facts. Do you know where to go to hunt for treasure from the famous pirate Blackbeard? Can you guess how fast a human cannonball can fly through the air? What's the average age of a video game player? Are you pop-culture pro enough to know what singer Taylor Swift did on her 18th birthday to show she was a good citizen?

Whether you're a fan of funny fads, an expert on exciting pop stars, or a wannabe wild weather tracker, get ready to stretch your smarts. If it's gross insects, the latest video games, or space travel that interest you, get ready. You're on your way to becoming one of the best young trivia masters!

Before you begin, here are a few helpful hints on how this book is organized. With many different kinds of quiz games inside, you can pick your favorites or tackle them all. In "True or False?" quizzes, guess whether the 30 theme-related statements are fact or fiction. Then flip to the answer pages to discover the many surprising answers. In "Map Mania!" quizzes, use maps to locate the places where the first explorers traveled, where fantastic animal fossils are found, or where thrill-seekers go to experience extreme adventures around the world. Multiple choice and more true-or-false questions throughout the book cover movie villains, rock-and-roll music, extreme sports, knights, dragons, presidents, national parks, scuba diving, Antarctica, food, bees, beaches, and oh so much more quiz whiz-ology! Each chapter ends with a "Game Show," where you'll find special photo questions and an extra-challenging "Ultimate Brain Buster."

Whether you take our *Quiz Whiz 2* challenge alone or with friends or family, answers to all the questions appear at the end of the book—just in case a few mighty questions short circuit your brain. Check answers for one quiz or all of the quizzes in a chapter. Tally your scores and discover which topics you'd like to learn more about! The best part about this book is that it doesn't matter whether anyone gets the answers right. Having fun together and learning new, cool stuff is the reward.

Time to begin your *Quiz Whiz 2* challenge, young brainiac. We can already see you getting smarter by the page!

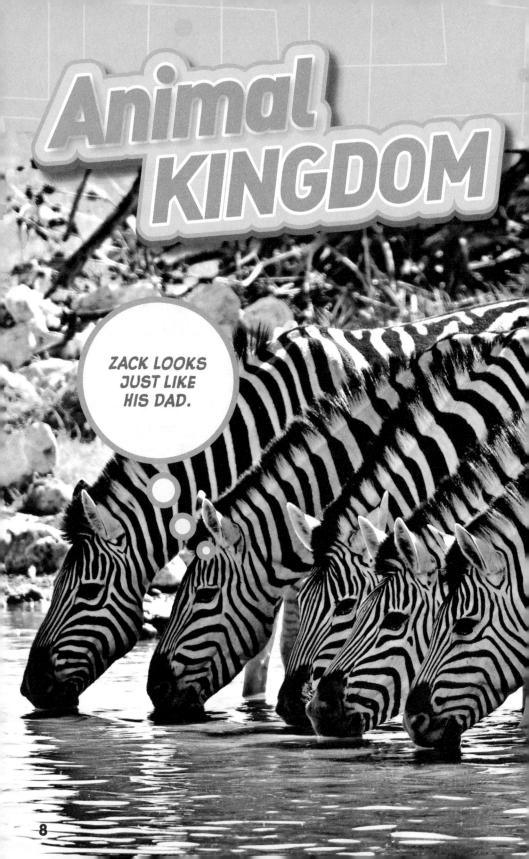

The WILD LIFE

1 Why do bats hang upside down?
- **a.** to hide from predators
- **b.** to scare off predators
- **c.** to conserve their energy
- **d.** to hear sounds better

BLACK FLYING-FOX BAT

2 **True or false?** The largest mammal is the blue whale.

3 Which is the slowest mammal on Earth?
- **a.** muskrat
- **b.** meerkat
- **c.** koala
- **d.** sloth

4 When does the hooded seal display its balloon-like "hood"?
- **a.** when it is sleeping
- **b.** when it is hungry
- **c.** when it is threatened
- **d.** when it is nursing its pups

5 **True or false?** Elephants are born blind.

6 Which is the wombat's closest relative?
- **a.** koala
- **b.** pig
- **c.** turtle
- **d.** cougar

WOMBAT

DALMATIAN

7 Where are a dog's sweat glands located?
a. in its mouth
b. the bottoms of its feet
c. behind its ears
d. in its nose

8 The red panda also goes by which name?
a. firefox
b. red beast
c. panda-monium
d. Kung-Fu Panda

9 Which of these animals likes to eat skunks?
a. dog
b. grizzly bear
c. eel
d. great horned owl

10 True or false? The platypus is the only mammal that lays eggs.

OKAPI

11 Which animal was considered extinct until the 1990s?
a. aye-aye
b. hairy-eared dwarf lemur
c. star-nosed mole
d. Asian tapir

12 To which animal is the okapi most closely related?
a. monkey
b. lion
c. giraffe
d. rhinoceros

CHECK YOUR ANSWERS ON PAGES 158–159.

CATCHING SOME ZZZs

1 Which animal is nocturnal, meaning it sleeps during the day and is awake at night?

a. turtle
b. bear
c. badger
d. rabbit

2 Experts can tell if an animal is hibernating, not sleeping, because it has _____.

a. a higher body temperature
b. a lower body temperature
c. open eyes
d. closed eyes

3 True or false? Tigers sleep next to their meals.

4 The albatross, a large seabird, can sleep while _____.

a. diving into water
b. laying an egg
c. eating
d. flying

5 What kinds of animals hibernate?

a. fish
b. amphibians
c. reptiles
d. all of the above

6 Most animals have a 24-hour sleep cycle, but snails have a sleep cycle every _____.

a. 2 to 3 days
b. 6 months
c. 3 years
d. 5 years

7 Which animal can hibernate while partially frozen?

a. frog
b. duck
c. bear
d. snake

8 True or false? Some birds sleep with one eye open.

9 How many hours a day does the average house cat sleep?

a. 5
b. 12
c. 16
d. 24

10 Which animal spends 80 percent of its **life asleep?**

a. elephant
b. horse
c. armadillo
d. giraffe

11 Which color does a green **tree frog** turn to hide from predators?

a. tan
b. blue
c. yellow
d. red

12 Why don't birds fall off branches when they sleep?

a. They are not fully asleep.
b. Their legs lock in place.
c. They perch on wide, flat branches.
d. Their breathing pattern helps them balance.

13 Which animal wears a **cocoon** of dead skin during hibernation?

a. African bullfrog
b. North American black bear
c. common housefly
d. snapping turtle

14 True or false? Crocodiles sleep with their mouths closed.

15 Which animals sleep for as long as humans do—about **8 hours**—and at night?

a. elephants
b. dolphins
c. koalas
d. pigs

HI, HONEY, I'M HOME!

1 How long have honeybees been producing honey?

a. 10 years
b. 1,000 years
c. 100,000 years
d. 10 million years

2 How many flowers must a hive of bees visit to produce an average jar of honey?

a. 2
b. 50
c. 2 million
d. 10 million

3 **True or false?** In ancient times, dead people were given honey cakes to take to the afterlife.

4 **True or false?** The queen bee collects the most pollen in a hive.

5 A queen honeybee usually lives for about_____.

a. 5 days
b. 5 weeks
c. 5 months
d. 5 years

6 An adult honeybee is about the size of a(n) _____.

a. human fingernail
b. quarter
c. iPhone
d. head of a pin

7 Why do honeybees gather together in a big ball, called a cluster?

a. to teach young bees to fly
b. to stay warm
c. to attack
d. to make a lot of honey quickly

14

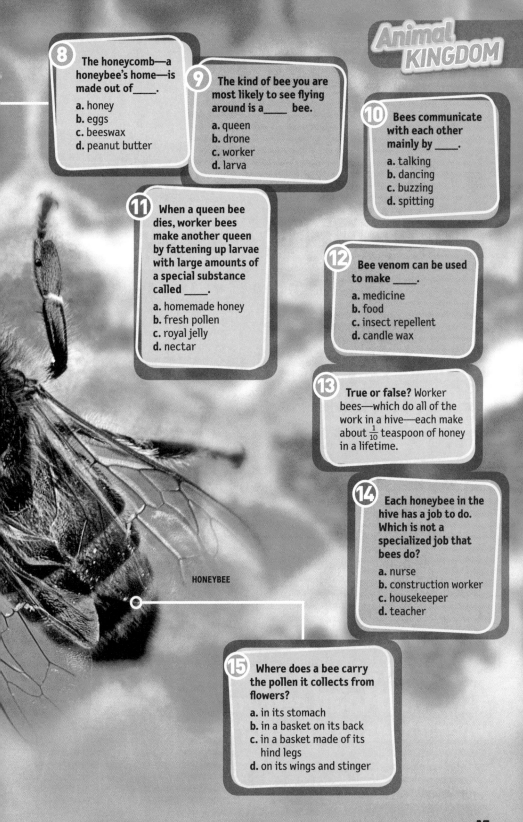

8 The honeycomb—a honeybee's home—is made out of____.
a. honey
b. eggs
c. beeswax
d. peanut butter

9 The kind of bee you are most likely to see flying around is a____ bee.
a. queen
b. drone
c. worker
d. larva

10 Bees communicate with each other mainly by ____.
a. talking
b. dancing
c. buzzing
d. spitting

11 When a queen bee dies, worker bees make another queen by fattening up larvae with large amounts of a special substance called ____.
a. homemade honey
b. fresh pollen
c. royal jelly
d. nectar

12 Bee venom can be used to make ____.
a. medicine
b. food
c. insect repellent
d. candle wax

13 **True or false?** Worker bees—which do all of the work in a hive—each make about $\frac{1}{10}$ teaspoon of honey in a lifetime.

14 Each honeybee in the hive has a job to do. Which is not a specialized job that bees do?
a. nurse
b. construction worker
c. housekeeper
d. teacher

HONEYBEE

15 Where does a bee carry the pollen it collects from flowers?
a. in its stomach
b. in a basket on its back
c. in a basket made of its hind legs
d. on its wings and stinger

CHECK YOUR ANSWERS ON PAGES 158–159.

AND NOW FOR MY NEXT TRICK...

1 What trick can **hummingbirds** do?

a. fly upside down and backward
b. lift objects heavier than themselves
c. grow a new set of wings
d. make honey like bees

2 From how far away can elephants still hear each other's **low-rumbling calls?**

a. 2 feet (.6 m)
b. 6 miles (10 km)
c. 81 miles (130 km)
d. 153 miles (246 km)

3 True or false? Crocodiles eat stones to help them grind and digest their food.

4 Which of the following is not a trick a **chameleon** can do?

a. move each of its eyes separately
b. change its color
c. hold its breath for several days
d. stretch its tongue longer than the size of its body

5 What crazy stunt does a **horned toad** perform when it feels threatened?

a. kick dirt at predators
b. shoot blood from its eyes
c. shoot poison from its tongue
d. change colors and hide

6 Which animal can grow up to **40 new** sets of teeth in its lifetime?

a. beaver
b. tarantula
c. alligator
d. snake

7 Each year, the purple frog (yes, it's really purple!) lives **above the ground** for only ____.

a. 2 days
b. 2 weeks
c. 5 weeks
d. 3 months

8 True or false? The deep-sea shrimp squirts its enemies with a glowing blue ooze.

9 Spitting spiders shoot a **sticky substance** at their prey to ____.

a. stun it
b. hold it down and eat it
c. blind it
d. add flavor

10 Which animal can change direction in midair while chasing its prey?

a. golden retriever
b. antelope
c. tabby cat
d. cheetah

11 How far can a **kangaroo leap?**

a. 3 feet (1 m)
b. 8 feet (2 m)
c. 44 feet (13 m)
d. 104 feet (32 m)

12 True or false? All spiders spin webs in the same pattern.

13 Which sea animal can dive over **6,600 feet** (2,010 m) below the surface of the water?

a. sperm whale
b. horseshoe crab
c. jellyfish
d. emperor penguin

What's for DINNER?

1. **Which animal eats both seeds and worms?**
   - **a.** chicken
   - **b.** cheetah
   - **c.** salmon
   - **d.** rabbit

2. **About how many hours a day does a panda spend eating?**
   - **a.** 6
   - **b.** 10
   - **c.** 12
   - **d.** 24

3. **Which animal eats some foods that are so tiny we can't see them?**
   - **a.** seal
   - **b.** hawk
   - **c.** raccoon
   - **d.** fish

4. **True or false?** Vampire bats don't really drink blood.

5. **An anaconda eats its prey whole. Which animal does an anaconda sometimes eat?**
   - **a.** eel
   - **b.** deer
   - **c.** horse
   - **d.** whale

ANACONDA

6. **The silky anteater is the world's smallest anteater. How many ants does it eat in one day?**
   - **a.** 50
   - **b.** 250
   - **c.** 700
   - **d.** 5,000

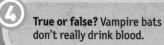

SILKY ANTEATER

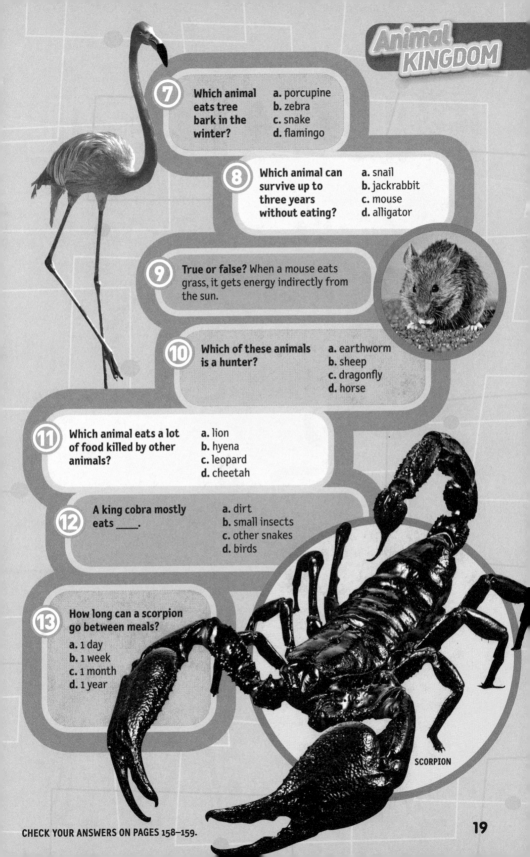

7 Which animal eats tree bark in the winter?
a. porcupine
b. zebra
c. snake
d. flamingo

8 Which animal can survive up to three years without eating?
a. snail
b. jackrabbit
c. mouse
d. alligator

9 **True or false?** When a mouse eats grass, it gets energy indirectly from the sun.

10 Which of these animals is a hunter?
a. earthworm
b. sheep
c. dragonfly
d. horse

11 Which animal eats a lot of food killed by other animals?
a. lion
b. hyena
c. leopard
d. cheetah

12 A king cobra mostly eats ____.
a. dirt
b. small insects
c. other snakes
d. birds

13 How long can a scorpion go between meals?
a. 1 day
b. 1 week
c. 1 month
d. 1 year

SCORPION

CHECK YOUR ANSWERS ON PAGES 158–159.

MAP MANIA!
PALS IN PERIL

The habitats of these animals are shrinking. Match each animal to the red dot on the map marking a region where it lives in the wild.

1 KOALA

2 KOMODO DRAGON

3 GIANT RIVER OTTER

4 RED-FRONTED GAZELLE

ARC

NORTH AMERICA

B

PACIFIC OCEAN

ATLAN OCEA

C ● ● D

SOUTH AMERICA

5 HYACINTH MACAW

Animal KINGDOM

6 CALIFORNIA CONDOR

7 POLAR BEAR

8 WHITE RHINOCEROS

9 RING-TAILED LEMUR

10 GRAY WOLF

OCEAN

E

EUROPE

ASIA

PACIFIC OCEAN

OCEANIA

F

AFRICA

G H

INDIAN OCEAN

I

AUSTRALIA

J

ANTARCTICA

CHECK YOUR ANSWERS ON PAGES 158–159.

21

Egg-cellent ANIMALS

1 Which animal lays the largest egg?

a. ostrich
b. turtle
c. bald eagle
d. chameleon

2 Crocodile eggs hatch after _____.

a. warming in the sun
b. the crocodile mother sits on them
c. being stored in a cave
d. floodwater covers them

3 What is it called when an insect or reptile crawls out of its own skin?

a. molting
b. relocating
c. weathering
d. hibernating

4 How many eggs does a female tuna lay at one time?

a. hundreds
b. thousands
c. millions
d. billions

5 Which animal's egg is often called a "mermaid's purse"?

a. seahorse
b. jellyfish
c. shark
d. octopus

6 Which animal is ready to hunt prey as soon as it hatches out of its egg?

a. tuna
b. bald eagle
c. Komodo dragon
d. piranha

7 Which animal does not hatch from an egg?

a. shark
b. whale
c. parrot
d. ladybug

8 Where does the cuckoo bird lay its eggs?

a. in another bird's nest
b. on the ground
c. near water
d. in a nest it makes from human trash

9 **What happens** if firefly eggs are disturbed before they hatch?

a. They hatch.
b. They glow.
c. They shake.
d. They squeak.

10 A **hummingbird egg** is about the size of a _____.

a. quarter
b. hummingbird
c. jellybean
d. nail head

11 **About how many** eggs does a female **monarch butterfly** lay in a lifetime?

a. 30
b. 300
c. 4,000
d. 10,000

12 **Which male animal carries eggs** in its pouch until they hatch?

a. kangaroo
b. seahorse
c. spider
d. frog

13 **True or false?** Flamingo eggs hatch only in the spring.

14 **What can baby turkeys** do as soon as they hatch?

a. lay eggs
b. jump
c. fly
d. walk

OSTRICH

CHECK YOUR ANSWERS ON PAGES 158–159.

GOING APE

1 **True or false?** Each gorilla's nose print is unique, like a human fingerprint.

2 The leader of a gorilla group is called a _____.
a. lowlander
b. boss
c. queen gorilla
d. silverback

3 A group of gorillas is called a _____.
a. gaggle
b. troop
c. flock
d. school

4 **True or false?** Gorillas eat mostly meat.

5 About how many mountain gorillas are left on Earth?

a. 90
b. 900
c. 9,000
d. 9 million

6 True or false? Gorillas use sticks to measure the depth of water.

7 Gorillas have a high domed head that _____.

a. supports large muscles for grinding food
b. holds an extra large brain
c. is used to crack open nuts
d. provides room for a mouth full of extra-large teeth

8 Which animal is the gorilla's closest relation?

a. spider monkey
b. brown bear
c. chimpanzee
d. sloth

9 True or false? Gorillas have the same number of teeth as humans.

10 Which of the following is not a real species of gorilla?

a. northern tree
b. eastern lowland
c. western lowland
d. Cross River

11 What body parts do monkeys have that gorillas do not?

a. tails
b. fingers
c. toes
d. knees

12 A captive gorilla named Koko was able to communicate with humans using what?

a. chalk and a blackboard
b. sign language
c. speech
d. toys

13 For how long does a young gorilla share a nest with its mother?

a. 1 to 2 days
b. 3 to 6 weeks
c. 4 to 6 years
d. 12 to 14 years

WESTERN LOWLAND
GORILLA

CHECK YOUR ANSWERS ON PAGES 158–159.

What's a BODY TO DO?

1 What does a lion use as feelers?
- **a.** eyelashes
- **b.** teeth
- **c.** whiskers
- **d.** claws

2 Which bird uses its beak to hook prey and tear it apart?
- **a.** hummingbird
- **b.** mallard duck
- **c.** parakeet
- **d.** snowy owl

3 **True or false?** Humans' sharpest teeth are named after dogs.

4 This dog breed is known for rescuing lost hikers in the deep snow of the Swiss Alps.
- **a.** golden retriever
- **b.** Chihuahua
- **c.** bloodhound
- **d.** Saint Bernard

5 Which body part does a mouse use to keep its balance?
- **a.** ear
- **b.** tongue
- **c.** tail
- **d.** leg

6 What does a mosquito use its antennae for?
- **a.** to see
- **b.** to hear
- **c.** to think
- **d.** to eat

7 Ducks' _____ feathers help them stay dry when swimming.

a. short
b. long
c. oily
d. light colored

8 **True or false?** Porcupines can shoot their quills at enemies.

PORCUPINE

9 Which animal has the best hearing?

a. tawny owl
b. earthworm
c. Galápagos giant tortoise
d. carrier pigeon

10 An elephant uses its trunk to do all of the following, except _____?

a. scare off predators
b. drink and wash
c. reach tall leaves
d. chew food

11 Which animal has webbing on its feet?

a. otter
b. lion
c. horse
d. parrot

12 **True or false?** A fly's eye contains many smaller eyes within it.

CHECK YOUR ANSWERS ON PAGES 158–159.

TRUE or FALSE?

Home Sweet Home

1 TREE FROGS CAN SPEND THEIR WHOLE LIVES IN A PLANT.

2 THERE ARE GLOW-IN-THE-DARK ANIMALS AT THE BOTTOM OF THE OCEAN.

3 ANTS CAN BE FOUND ON EVERY CONTINENT IN THE WORLD.

4 POLAR BEARS AND PENGUINS SHARE THE SAME HABITAT.

5 A SINGLE ANT COMMUNITY CAN EXTEND OVER THOUSANDS OF MILES.

6 THERE'S A FISH THAT CAN SURVIVE OUT OF WATER FOR MORE THAN TWO MONTHS.

7 SKUNKS LEAVE THEIR HOME, OR DEN, ONLY DURING THE DAY.

8 UNDERGROUND ANIMAL HOMES ARE CALLED NESTS.

9 SOME BIRDS MIGRATE FROM THE UNITED STATES TO THE AMAZON RAIN FOREST IN SOUTH AMERICA.

10 FEMALE MOUNTAIN GOATS STAY WITH THEIR CHILDREN, WHILE MALES LIVE ALONE.

11 THE ARCTIC FOX CHANGES COLORS TO MATCH ITS WINTER AND SUMMER SURROUNDINGS.

12 MOST ANIMALS THAT DWELL IN CAVES HAVE EXCELLENT EYESIGHT.

13 SOME FISH CAN SURVIVE UNDER MUD INSTEAD OF IN WATER.

14 WOLVES PREFER TO LIVE ALONE.

15 A NEW SPECIES OF MOSQUITO CAN BE FOUND ONLY IN THE SUBWAY SYSTEM IN LONDON, ENGLAND.

16 THERE'S AN OWL SPECIES THAT NESTS INSIDE A GIANT CACTUS.

17 NAKED MOLE RATS BURROW IN UNDERGROUND COLONIES IN AFRICA.

18 THOUSANDS OF STRAY DOGS MAKE THEIR HOMES IN MOSCOW'S SUBWAY SYSTEM.

19 SOME WATERBIRDS FIND DINNER ON THE BACKS OF HIPPOS.

20 THE DESERT IS HOME TO MOST TOUCANS.

21 GRAY FOXES MAKE THEIR HOMES IN THE TREETOPS.

22 SOME SCORPIONS LIVE IN CITIES.

23 THOUSANDS OF WILD BOARS ROAM FREE IN THE CITY OF BERLIN, GERMANY.

24 SOME KINDS OF INSECTS MAKE THEIR NESTS IN TREE BARK.

25 ANTS RELOCATE THEIR EGGS FROM A BIRTHING CHAMBER TO AN INCUBATOR AFTER THEY ARE HATCHED.

26 THE ROADRUNNER BIRD FEATURED IN THE CLASSIC *ROAD RUNNER* CARTOONS IS NOT A REAL BIRD SPECIES.

27 ABOUT A QUARTER OF ALL MARINE CREATURES DEPEND ON CORAL REEFS.

28 THERE ARE SNAKES IN ANTARCTICA.

29 FERRETS EAT PRAIRIE DOGS AND THEN TAKE OVER THEIR BURROWS.

30 PORCUPINES AND ALLIGATORS DWELL IN THE SAME CLIMATES.

CHECK YOUR ANSWERS ON PAGES 158–159.

1 Which animal protects itself by rolling up into a ball?
a. three-banded armadillo
b. raccoon
c. grizzly bear
d. chuckwalla

2 Which animal's brain can fit into half a tablespoon (7 mL)?
a. alligator
b. chimpanzee
c. hedgehog
d. elephant

3 A group of bees is called a _____.
a. litter
b. clutch
c. squad
d. swarm

4 An ostrich's eyeball is the size of its _____.
a. stomach
b. beak
c. brain
d. heart

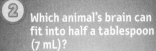

5 A skunk can shoot its spray up to _____.
a. 5 inches (12 cm)
b. 2 feet (0.6 m)
c. 10 feet (3 m)
d. 682 feet (207 m)

6 TRUE OR FALSE?
The male platypus can sting its enemies.

7 Which of these snakes is poisonous?
a. king cobra
b. corn snake
c. garter snake
d. green snake

8 How far can a sloth move in one minute?
a. 2 feet (0.6 m)
b. 5 feet (1.5 m)
c. 10 feet (3 m)
d. 20 feet (6 m)

9 This animal can run just as fast backward as it can forward.
a. naked mole rat
b. chicken
c. hippo
d. penguin

10

There is a squirrel with wings.

11 Which of these animals migrates thousands of miles each year?
a. arctic tern
b. gray whale
c. monarch butterfly
d. all of the above

12 Which animal's tail can detach to help it escape from a predator?
a. kangaroo
b. gerbil
c. rabbit
d. dormouse

13 Which of these creatures is *not* an insect?

a.
butterfly

b.
cricket

c.
spider

d.
beetle

14 Dalmatians are born without their _____.
a. black spots
b. tails
c. fur
d. sense of smell

15

ULTIMATE BRAIN BUSTER

CAN YOU IDENTIFY THE ANIMAL IN THIS PICTURE?

CHECK YOUR ANSWERS ON PAGES 158–159.

What on EARTH?

COAST TO COAST

1 All of the world's oceans cover how much of Earth's surface?

a. 20 percent
b. 55 percent
c. 71 percent
d. 91 percent

2 True or false? Horses first came to Australia by ship with the arrival of Irish and British settlers.

3 What is the name of a dangerous current that can pull swimmers away from a shore?

a. tsunami
b. rip current
c. cross wave
d. neap tide

4 What is a mangrove?

a. a large seashell
b. a bitter fruit shaped like a human head
c. a tree that can grow on sandy seashores
d. a tool used to harvest coconuts

5 What object in space is responsible for high and low tides?

a. moon
b. sun
c. Neptune
d. tidal satellite

6 True or false? Sand dunes are found only in coastal areas.

7 True or false? Sea cliffs are created by waves pounding the lower portion of a rock wall.

8 Which of the following seabirds can swim but not fly?

a. seagull
b. penguin
c. crane
d. puffin

9 If all the world's coastlines were added together, how many miles (km) would they stretch across?

a. 5 miles (8 km)
b. 221,208 miles (356,000 km)
c. 546,000 miles (879,000 km)
d. 10 million miles (16 million km)

10 What is the name of the deepest place in the ocean—located in the Pacific?

a. Enormous Giant Ocean Trench
b. Challenger Deep
c. Deep Pacific Trench Coat
d. Oceanic Southern Trench

11 True or false? There are more grains of sand on Earth than stars in the sky.

12 Coastal grasses help ____.

a. give sand dunes a pretty color
b. pull the sea inland
c. stabilize sand dunes
d. hide sea monsters

13 The most powerful light in a lighthouse today can be seen approximately how far out at sea?

a. 2 feet (.6 m)
b. 10 miles (16 km)
c. 25 miles (40.2 km)
d. all the way across the ocean

COASTAL VIEW OF THE TASMAN SEA BETWEEN AUSTRALIA AND NEW ZEALAND

14 True or false? Canada has a longer coastline than Poland.

15 Seaweed is a type of algae that grows in the water. It has been used for ____.

a. wrapping sushi
b. fertilizing crops
c. polishing shoes
d. all of the above

CHECK YOUR ANSWERS ON PAGES 159–160.

MARK YOUR CALENDAR

1 The mysterious structure of **Stonehenge** is thought to be as old as the _____.

a. sun
b. Grand Canyon
c. Egyptian pyramids
d. Leaning Tower of Pisa

2 What type of competition takes place at the **annual Wimbledon Championships?**

a. tennis
b. skydiving
c. swimming
d. extreme biking

3 In which celebration is it traditional for people to dance through the streets wearing a **dragon costume?**

a. Midnight Festival
b. Mardi Gras
c. Presidents' Day
d. Chinese New Year

4 During the Holi holiday in India, people celebrate by throwing what at each other?

a. colored water paint, and powder
b. pies
c. paper money
d. fruit

5 True or false? Wrapping a pole with colorful ribbons is an important part of May Day celebrations.

6 If you have triskaidekaphobia, you have a fear of _____.

a. math
b. the number 13
c. tricycles
d. the number 3

STONEHENGE

7 What is a **leap year?**

a. a year honoring the game of leapfrog

b. a year in which an extra day is added to February

c. a year in which a day is subtracted from April

d. a year celebrating the kangaroo in Australia

8 True or false? A day on Earth is longer than a day on Mars.

10 True or false? On April 1 in France, people play pranks by sticking a paper fish to the backs of their unsuspecting victims.

9 What is it called when a **second full moon appears** in one calendar month?

a. Daylight Savings Time

b. an extra moon month

c. a blue moon

d. a lunar month

12 Where could you attend the Monkey Buffet Festival in which monkeys are presented with a table filled with fruits and vegetables?

a. Thailand

b. New Zealand

c. California

d. Chile

11 If it is summer and you can still see the **sun at midnight**, you may be _____.

a. in Puerto Rico

b) in Norway

c. near the equator

d. in a time warp

13 Thousands of people attend a **festival in Spain** in order to hurl what at each other?

a. mud

b. raw eggs

c. tomatoes

d. snowballs

Be a Good SPORT!

1 True or false? In England, competitors from around the world race down a steep hill chasing giant wheels of cheese.

2 Which of these is a real sport?
a. chess-boxing (alternating rounds of chess and boxing)
b. puzzle-hiking (hike into a dark cave and put together a puzzle)
c. rocket science–rafting (raft 100 miles [161 km] out to sea and launch a toy rocket)
d. opera singing–mountain climbing (climb a mountain and sing a note that breaks glass)

3 True or false? In blo-ball, players blow the ball back and forth between them.

4 What sports record do people try to break at the Bonneville Salt Flats in Utah, U.S.A.?
a. longest quidditch game
b. fastest motorized land vehicle
c. wettest water balloon toss
d. fastest horse-pulled covered wagon

5 In 2002, Lloyd Scott broke the world record for the slowest marathon time, by running the London Marathon wearing a ____.
a. Darth Vader mask
b. giant pumpkin costume
c. 130-pound (59-kg) diving suit
d. pair of shoes made of cement

6 A popular Southeast Asian sport, called sepaktakraw—a cross between volleyball and soccer—uses a ball made of ____.
a. marshmallows and peanut butter
b. woven palm stems
c. beehives
d. ice

What on EARTH?

7 **True or false?** Tug-of-war was once an Olympic sport.

8 A competitive skydiver can fall at speeds greater than ____.
a. 2 feet per hour (.6 m/hr)
b. 5 miles per hour (8 kph)
c. 330 miles per hour (531 kph)
d. 800 miles per hour (1,287 kph)

9 Which piece of equipment is used in the sport of lacrosse?
a. b. c. d.

10 Which of these sports is played on horseback?
a. curling
b. competitive kite-flying
c. gymnastics
d. polo

11 In badminton, what do players hit across a net?
a. a feathered cork
b. a wiffle ball
c. a balloon
d. a billiard ball

BADMINTON MATCH

12 Which of the following is an actual sport?
a. toe wrestling
b. extreme ironing
c. underwater hockey
d. all of the above

TRUE or FALSE?
ON LOCATION

1 THE VIEW FROM PIKES PEAK IN COLORADO, U.S.A., WAS THE INSPIRATION FOR THE SONG "AMERICA THE BEAUTIFUL."

2 THE AMAZON RIVER IS IN EASTERN AFRICA.

3 THE FIRST MAN TO SUCCESSFULLY FLY OVER THE SOUTH POLE FIRST EXPLORED ANTARCTICA IN THE YEAR 1975.

4 THE FIRST BABY WAX FIGURE CREATED FOR MADAME TUSSAUDS WAX MUSEUM WAS SHILOH JOLIE-PITT, DAUGHTER OF ANGELINA JOLIE AND BRAD PITT.

5 THE FAMOUS PAINTING *MONA LISA* WAS ONCE STOLEN FROM A PARIS MUSEUM.

6 MOUNT FUJI, THE HIGHEST MOUNTAIN IN JAPAN, IS AN ACTIVE VOLCANO.

7 MORE THAN A THOUSAND ELEPHANTS HELPED BUILD THE TAJ MAHAL, A FAMOUS BUILDING IN INDIA.

8 THE CITY OF VANCOUVER, CANADA, HAS NEVER HOSTED THE WINTER OLYMPICS.

9 THE FAMOUS GREAT SPHINX STATUE IN EGYPT HAS THE FACE OF A LION AND THE BODY OF A WOMAN.

10 THE BRITISH OPEN IS THE WORLD'S NEWEST GOLF CHAMPIONSHIP.

11 WOODEN SHOES ARE A POPULAR SOUVENIR FOR TOURISTS IN GREENLAND.

12 THE FORBIDDEN CITY IS LOCATED IN BEIJING, CHINA.

13 MANY PEOPLE CONSIDERED THE EIFFEL TOWER TO BE AN EYESORE WHEN IT WAS FIRST BUILT IN PARIS, FRANCE.

14 THERE'S A HEART-SHAPED ISLAND OFF THE COAST OF CROATIA.

15 THERE'S AN UNDERWATER MUSEUM IN MEXICO.

16 THE UNITED STATES HAS TEN GREAT LAKES.

17 TINKER BELL, THE FAIRY FROM *PETER PAN*, FLIES OVER WALT DISNEY WORLD EVERY NIGHT BEFORE THE FIREWORKS SHOW STARTS.

18 YOU CAN TRAVEL AROUND THE CITY OF VENICE, ITALY, BY BOAT.

19 YOU CAN STAY IN A LODGE IN ASIA THAT'S SHAPED LIKE AN ELEPHANT.

20 VISITORS TO THE SWEETWATER RATTLESNAKE ROUNDUP IN TEXAS, U.S.A., CAN SEE A RATTLESNAKE BEING "MILKED."

21 ROME, ITALY'S, SOCCER TEAM PLAYS HOME GAMES IN THE ANCIENT ARENA CALLED THE COLOSSEUM.

22 BUILDINGS IN A SPANISH CITY WERE PAINTED BLUE TO PROMOTE THE MOVIE *THE SMURFS*.

23 WASHINGTON'S NOSE ON MOUNT RUSHMORE IN SOUTH DAKOTA, U.S.A., IS LONGER THAN AN AVERAGE SCHOOL BUS.

24 YOU WOULD BE LIKELY TO HEAR THE GREETING "ALOHA!" IN THE FIJI ISLANDS.

25 ACCORDING TO LEGEND, ST. PATRICK WAS KNOWN FOR RIDDING IRELAND OF SPIDERS.

26 THE HIGHEST WATERSLIDE IN THE WORLD IS THE "INSANO" IN BRAZIL.

27 CAVE PAINTINGS FOUND IN SPAIN ARE BELIEVED TO BE MORE THAN 40,000 YEARS OLD!

28 IN THE HARRY POTTER BOOKS, HOGWARTS SCHOOL OF WITCHCRAFT AND WIZARDRY IS LOCATED IN ENGLAND.

29 IF YOU TRAVELED TO ICELAND IN JUNE, IT WOULD BE DARK ALL DAY LONG.

30 THE SAHARA DESERT COVERS AN AREA SLIGHTLY LARGER THAN AUSTRALIA.

CHECK YOUR ANSWERS ON PAGES 159–160.

41

Let's Talk TRADITION!

1 Legend has it that kissing the Blarney Stone in Ireland gives you _____.
- **a.** chicken pox
- **b.** the gift of gab
- **c.** a headache
- **d.** a pocketful of pebbles

2 **True or false?** It is rude to touch anyone on top of the head in Vietnam.

HAGGIS

3 In Scotland, haggis is a traditional food. What is haggis?
- **a.** hamburger baked inside a large noodle
- **b.** chopped liver inside a pastry shell
- **c.** sausage cooked inside a sheep's stomach
- **d.** a Scottish word for meatball

4 What is the name of the traditional instrument played by the Aboriginal people of Australia?
- **a.** singing stick
- **b.** loka loka shmoo
- **c.** flutaphone
- **d.** didgeridoo

5 **True or false?** In some parts of the world, it is considered rude to speak to someone when your hands are in your pockets.

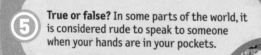

6 The Haka is a war dance that members of a New Zealand team perform before what kind of game?
a. soccer
b. chess
c. rugby
d. duck duck goose

HAKA DANCE

7 True or false? Making the strangest face possible is a custom called gurning in England. There's even a competition for it!

8 Traditional writing in ancient Egypt was made up of pictures called ____.
a. hieroglyphs
b. magic drawings
c. alphapics
d. Etch A Sketch

9 True or false? Fortune cookies were invented in China.

10 Originally Swiss shepherds yodeled to do what?
a. make extra money
b. frighten away wolves
c. order food
d. communicate with their domesticated animals and each other

11 True or false? In Denmark, people celebrate the New Year by throwing dishes at their friends' houses.

12 The Italian game tamburello, named after a musical instrument, is similar to tennis but uses what instead of a racket?
a. pizza pan
b. tambourine
c. shovel
d. cello

CHECK YOUR ANSWERS ON PAGES 159–160.

TAKE ME TO YOUR LEADER

1 Moctezuma was the leader from 1502–1520 of the Aztec people near what city that still exists today?

a. Mexico City, Mexico
b. Paris, France
c. Phoenix, Arizona, U.S.A.
d. Tokyo, Japan

2 Buckingham Palace in London, England, is home to which famous person?

a. British prime minister
b. William Shakespeare
c. Queen Elizabeth II
d. J.K. Rowling

3 True or false? Russian rulers used to receive a single chocolate egg as a gift on Easter.

4 Which U.S. president grew a beard after receiving a letter from a little girl suggesting he would look better with one?

a. Thomas Jefferson
b. Abraham Lincoln
c. Harry Truman
d. Bill Clinton

5 In 2006, the prime minister of Japan visited the home of what American music legend?

a. Phillip Phillips
b. Elvis Presley
c. Lady Gaga
d. Justin Bieber

6 True or false? At the age of 42, Theodore Roosevelt was the youngest U.S. president to ever take office.

7 The Chinese government is known for giving what gifts to world leaders as a **gesture of goodwill?**

a. new cars
b. silver chopsticks
c. gold-plated iPhones
d. pandas

8 Former British prime minister John Major once sold _____.

a. Roboraptors
b. Krispy Kreme donuts
c. garden gnomes
d. carrots

9 The mummy of **Tutankhamun**, known as King Tut, was found inside a coffin made of what?

a. marble
b. gold
c. silver
d. bone

10 **True or false?** China's last ruling emperor was almost three years old when he took the throne.

11 **True or false?** Shogun is a title given to a military ruler in Germany.

AZTEC RUINS IN MEXICO

A Capital IDEA!

1 The town of Bloomer, Wisconsin, U.S.A., calls itself the Jump Rope Capital of the World because ____.

a. the mayor invented the jump rope
b. it has the world's thinnest jump rope
c. it hosts a yearly jump rope contest
d. it is home to a famous cat that can jump rope

2 The Angora cat is named after which capital city?

a. Paris, France
b. Berlin, Germany
c. Oslo, Norway
d. Ankara, Turkey

ANGORA CAT

3 This capital city is situated on the slopes of a volcano.

a. Quito, Ecuador
b. Dublin, Ireland
c. Washington, D.C., U.S.A.
d. Abuja, Nigeria

4 **True or false?** South Africa is the only country with three capital cities.

STATUE OF ROMULUS, REMUS, AND THE WOLF

5 According to legend, what capital city was founded by Romulus and Remus, twins who were cared for by a wolf?

a. Moscow, Russia
b. Rome, Italy
c. Hanoi, Vietnam
d. Seoul, South Korea

6 Red Square, once a seat of communist power, is located in which capital city?

a. Havana, Cuba
b. Madrid, Spain
c. Moscow, Russia
d. Washington, D.C., U.S.A.

7 **True or false?** Mexico City is the oldest city in North America.

8 Ottawa, Canada, is home to the world's longest skating rink, which is ____ long.

a. 4 feet (1.2 m)
b. 1 mile (1.6 km)
c. 5 miles (7.8 km)
d. 80 miles (128 km)

MOUNT FUJI

9 From which capital city can you see Mount Fuji?

a. Nassau, Bahamas
b. Vienna, Austria
c. London, England, U.K.
d. Tokyo, Japan

10 What city is the world's southernmost capital?

a. Reykjavik, Iceland
b. Wellington, New Zealand
c. Canberra, Australia
d. Brasília, Brazil

11 **True or false?** George Washington was the first president to live in the White House in the U.S. capital, Washington, D.C.

THE WHITE HOUSE

CHECK YOUR ANSWERS ON PAGES 159–160.

MAP MANIA!
GREAT ADVENTURE

① ZAMBEZI RIVER

This wild river draws white-water rafters from all over the world. On what continent can it be found?

a. Africa
b. North America
c. Asia
d. South America

② ALASKA, U.S.A.

Which annual race covers more than a thousand miles (1,600 km) and crosses two mountain ranges in this U.S. state?

a. New York Marathon
b. Olympics
c. The Tour de France
d. Iditarod Sled Dog Race

③ ANTARCTICA

What animals might you see on a trip to this continent?

a. whales
b. penguins
c. seals
d. all of the above

④ GUADALUPE ISLAND, MEXICO

Thrill-seekers can view sharks from underwater cages off the coast of this island, located in what body of water?

a. Atlantic Ocean
b. Gulf of Mexico
c. Pacific Ocean
d. Red Sea

Adventure-seekers travel the world to climb, dive, race, raft, and more! Find out how much you know about these thrilling adventures. Then match each adventure to the correct location on the map.

⑤ MOUNT EVEREST

Mountain climbers who want to conquer Mount Everest—the highest place on Earth—head to what Asian mountain range?

a. Andes
b. Canadian Rockies
c. Alps
d. Himalaya

⑥ AUSTRALIA

Cowboy types can saddle up for a nearly weeklong cattle drive across what rugged landscape in Australia?

a. Badlands
b. Outback
c. Never Go Back
d. Yukon

⑦ GALÁPAGOS ISLANDS

The Galápagos Islands, a popular spot for snorkelers, are located off the coast of what country?

a. Saudi Arabia
b. Ecuador
c. Mozambique
d. Cambodia

ARCTIC OCEAN

EUROPE

ASIA

AFRICA

PACIFIC OCEAN

INDIAN OCEAN

D AUSTRALIA

B

F

G ANTARCTICA

8–14 **MATCH EACH OF THESE** PLACES TO THE RED MARKER THAT SHOWS ITS CORRECT LOCATION ON THE MAP.

GAME SHOW

ULTIMATE EARTHLY CHALLENGE

1 Which of the following countries is landlocked?
a. Switzerland
b. Turkey
c. Peru
d. Finland

2 **TRUE OR FALSE?**
Glaciers are not found near the equator.

3 What is another name for the fruit known as the kiwi?
a. Boston banana
b. Chinese gooseberry
c. New Zealand melon
d. Chihuahua dog fruit

4 This animal's name is Greek for "river horse."
a. hippogriff
b. hippopotamus
c. unicorn
d. rhinoceros

5 The London Eye is a fancy _____.
a. spy camera
b. subway
c. telescope
d. Ferris wheel

6 What is a "snickerdoodle"?
a. a hat worn in Canada
b. the name for a pencil in Mexico
c. a cookie that originated in Germany
d. a fruit tree in India

7 **TRUE OR FALSE?**
The poisonous pufferfish is eaten by some people in the world.

What is "hurling"?
a. an Irish sport in which players use a hurley stick to hit a ball into a net
b. a medical condition that makes people sick to their stomachs
c. an Australian word that means "making soup"
d. a British video game in which monsters throw up

 Which famous place below is located in Italy?

a.
Eiffel Tower

b.
Empire State Building

c.
Leaning Tower of Pisa

d.
Sydney Opera House

 What country grows more strawberries than any other?
a. Mexico
b. Iceland
c. Saudi Arabia
d. United States

 A queen ruled this state before it was taken over as a U.S. territory in 1893.
a. Alaska
b. New Mexico
c. Hawaii
d. Florida

Famous athlete Bjorn Borg from Sweden, who won Wimbledon five years in a row, is known for what sport?
a. archery
b. tennis
c. ice hockey
d. swimming

 TRUE OR FALSE?
Elephants in Africa are larger than elephants in Asia.

The Red Sea probably gets its name from what?
a. red rafts that kids float on
b. the reflection from nearby red cliffs
c. red algae in the water
d. a sunken ship that spilled red paint

 ULTIMATE BRAIN BUSTER WHAT CITY IS KNOWN FOR ITS RED DOUBLE-DECKER BUSES?

a.
Oslo, Norway

b.
Moscow, Russia

c.
Rio de Janeiro, Brazil

d.
London, England, U.K.

CHECK YOUR ANSWERS ON PAGES 159–160.

Pop Culture

THE PENGUINS OF MADAGASCAR IS A POPULAR TV SHOW, BUT IN REAL LIFE, PENGUINS ARE NOWHERE TO BE FOUND ON THAT ISLAND, WHICH SITS OFF THE COAST OF AFRICA. RATHER, THE ANIMALS MAKE THEIR HOME FARTHER SOUTH, ALONG THE COAST OF SOUTH AFRICA.

THE PENGUINS OF MADAGASCAR

Kid TV

LEON G. THOMAS, AVAN JOGIA, ELIZABETH GILLIES, AND VICTORIA JUSTICE FROM THE HIT TV SHOW *VICTORIOUS*

1 Skipper and Kowalski are characters in which TV show?

a. *Victorious*
b. *Transformers*
c. *The Penguins of Madagascar*
d. *Regular Show*

2 What kind of character is Roger in *American Dad!*?

a. a dog
b. a rabbit
c. an alien
d. a robot

3 Tori Vega on the TV show *Victorious* has a talent in which of the following areas?

a. music
b. math
c. sports
d. science

SPONGEBOB WITH PATRICK STAR

4 Who is Sandy Cheeks in *SpongeBob SquarePants*?

a. a squirrel from Texas
b. a karate expert
c. a scientist
d. all of the above

5 What is the dog's name in the cartoon *Garfield*?

a. Odie
b. Benji
c. Arbuckle
d. Woofie Woof

6 In *iCarly*, who is Lewbert?

a. Freddie's uncle
b. Carly's doorman
c. T-Bo's boss
d. Gibby's brother

7 What do the football players in *Glee* throw on the members of the glee club?

a. fruit salad
b. orange juice
c. ice water
d. slushies

THE CAST OF *GLEE*

8 What is the name of Charlie's older sister in *Good Luck Charlie*?

a. PJ
b. Gabe
c. Teddy
d. Toby

9 In the show *Phineas and Ferb*, what is the relationship between the boys Phineas and Ferb?

a. neighbors
b. stepbrothers
c. cousins
d. friends

10 What is Mordecai in *Regular Show*?

a. a blue jay
b. a lollipop
c. a robin
d. a ghost

11 Who's Mike Baxter's boss in *Last Man Standing*?

a. Nancy
b. Christoph
c. Boyd
d. Ed

PHINEAS
AND FERB

12 Why does evil Master Xandred want to flood the Sanzu River with human tears in *Power Rangers Samurai*?

a. to build an army of Nighloks
b. to escape into the human world and take over
c. to capture Red Ranger Jayden
d. to heal his battle wounds

13 What valuable skill does *A.N.T. Farm* character Olive have on this TV show?

a. musical genius
b. athletic talent
c. photographic memory
d. good with computers

CHECK YOUR ANSWERS ON PAGES 161–162.

Famous VILLAINS

1 In the movie *The Wizard of Oz*, what does the Wicked Witch of the West say to Dorothy before disappearing in a puff of smoke? "I'll get you, ____"

a. my pet!
b. my pretty!
c. my dear!
d. my darling!

2 Which of these superheroes battled the Joker?

a. Batman
b. Superman
c. Iron Man
d. Captain America

3 **True or false?** Gandalf is Frodo's enemy in the movie *The Lord of the Rings: The Fellowship of the Ring*.

HARRY POTTER

4 Who is called "He-Who-Must-Not-Be-Named" in the *Harry Potter* movie series?

a. Tom Marvolo Riddle
b. The Dark Lord
c. Lord Voldemort
d. all of the above

DARTH VADER

5 In the movie *Superman*, what is villain Lex Luthor's main goal?

a. kidnap Robin
b. take over the world
c. steal the Batmobile
d. keep Superman busy

6 In the *Star Wars* movies, Darth Vader is the father of whom?

a. Han Solo
b. Luke Skywalker
c. Princess Leia
d. b and c

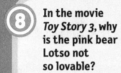

Pop Culture

7 How does the jealous queen try to kill Snow White?
- **a.** She has her look in a mirror.
- **b.** She gives her a poisoned apple.
- **c.** She locks her in a tower.
- **d.** She turns her into a dwarf.

8 In the movie *Toy Story 3*, why is the pink bear Lotso not so lovable?
- **a.** He makes new toys suffer.
- **b.** He wants to bury broken toys.
- **c.** He wants to close Sunnyside Daycare.
- **d.** He writes mean notes to children.

9 In *101 Dalmatians*, from whom does Cruella de Vil steal puppies?
- **a.** Roger and Anita
- **b.** Pongo and Perdita
- **c.** Horace and Jasper
- **d.** a and b

11 **True or false?** Gollum in *The Lord of the Rings* got his name from his Hobbit family.

10 Dr. Curt Connors becomes what villain in the movie *The Amazing Spider-Man*?
- **a.** The Lizard
- **b.** Green Goblin
- **c.** Doc Ock
- **d.** Hobgoblin

12 In *The Lion King*, what is the main goal of Scar?
- **a.** to be king of Pride Rock
- **b.** to trick Simba
- **c.** to create a stampede
- **d.** to train more hyenas

13 In the movie *Cinderella*, what is the meanest thing that the stepmother does to Cinderella?
- **a.** She yells at the prince.
- **b.** She shows no love to Cinderella.
- **c.** She rides in the pumpkin.
- **d.** She expects servants to clean for her.

GOLLUM

14 In *Matilda*, what do Matilda's classmates do to the bullying headmistress Agatha Trunchbull after Matilda's magical powers scare her?
- **a.** They report Trunchbull to the police.
- **b.** They complain to their parents.
- **c.** They pelt Trunchbull with food.
- **d.** They protest outside of school.

TRUE or FALSE?

Movie Mania!

1 IN *THE LIGHTNING THIEF*, PERCY JACKSON MUST MAKE PEACE BETWEEN HIS MOTHER, ZEUS, AND THOR.

2 THE EIGHT *HARRY POTTER* MOVIES ARE AMONG THE TOP MONEYMAKING FILMS IN THE WORLD.

3 IN *DIARY OF A WIMPY KID: DOG DAYS*, GREG WANTS TO BE IN HIS DAD'S PRETEND CIVIL WAR BATTLE, SO HE TRIES TO GROW A BEARD TO LOOK LIKE ABRAHAM LINCOLN.

4 IN *PARANORMAN*, NORMAN'S SPECIAL TALENT IS SPEAKING TO THE DEAD.

5 IN *BRAVE*, SCOTTISH PRINCESS MERIDA HAS A FIGHT WITH HER MOTHER BECAUSE SHE DOES NOT WANT TO ACT LIKE A TYPICAL PRINCESS.

6 IN *TRANSFORMERS*, THE DECEPTICONS USE INFORMATION ON THE GLASSES OF EXPLORER ARCHIBALD WITWICKY TO LOCATE THE ALLSPARK.

7 IN THE MOVIE *MADAGASCAR 3: EUROPE'S MOST WANTED*, ALEX, MARTY, MELMAN, AND GLORIA BOARD A SHIP AND CLAIM TO BE CIRCUS ANIMALS TO GET BACK TO NEW YORK.

8 IN *THE SEA OF MONSTERS*, PERCY JACKSON MUST FIND THE LOST CITY OF ATLANTIS TO SAVE CAMP HALF-BLOOD FROM BEING DESTROYED.

9 AT THE BEGINNING OF *ICE AGE: CONTINENTAL DRIFT*, SCRAT TRIES TO BURY HIS ACORN IN THE ICE AND CAUSES THE LAND TO BREAK INTO THE SEVEN CONTINENTS.

10 IN THE MOVIE *THE LORAX*, THE ONCE-LER FINALLY UNDERSTANDS THE MESSAGE THE LORAX LEAVES FOR HIM AND THEN GIVES THE LAST TRUFFULA SEED TO TED.

11 IN THE MOVIE *GULLIVER'S TRAVELS*, BEN STILLER PLAYS THE PART OF GULLIVER.

12 THE PIRATE CAPTAIN IN *THE PIRATES! BAND OF MISFITS* WANTS TO WIN THE PIRATE OF THE YEAR AWARD MORE THAN ANYTHING ELSE IN THE WORLD.

13 IN *THE ODD LIFE OF TIMOTHY GREEN*, TIMOTHY GREEN GROWS LEAVES ON HIS BODY.

14 *TOYS IN THE ATTIC* IS A MOVIE ABOUT TOYS THAT BUILD A BOAT AND SAIL AWAY.

15 THE CHARACTERS BRUCE, ANCHOR, AND CHUM ARE ALL SHARKS IN *FINDING NEMO*.

16 THE *AVENGERS* INCLUDE SUPERHEROES IRON MAN, THOR, THE HULK, AND CAPTAIN MARVEL.

17 IN *CARS 2*, LIGHTNING McQUEEN AND MATER TRAVEL TO TOKYO, JAPAN, FOR THE WORLD GRAND PRIX CAR RACE.

18 *THE LORD OF THE RINGS* MOVIES WERE FILMED IN NEW ZEALAND.

19 *THE SPY NEXT DOOR*, STARRING JACKIE CHAN, IS A COMEDY ABOUT A SPY NAMED BOB HO, WHOSE REAL NAME ISN'T BOB HO.

20 CAPTAIN AMERICA HAS NO REAL SUPERPOWERS.

21 IN *TRON: LEGACY*, SAM FLYNN TELEPORTS HIMSELF TO AN OUTER GALAXY.

22 THE STORY OF *KUNG FU PANDA* TAKES PLACE IN JAPAN.

23 IN *UP*, CARL'S HOUSE IS LIFTED OFF THE GROUND BY A TORNADO.

24 IN *IRON MAN*, TONY STARK REVEALS THAT IRON MAN IS A COMPUTERIZED ROBOT.

25 DRE PARKER LEARNS IN *THE KARATE KID* THAT A POWERFUL PUNCH IS THE KEY TO WINNING RESPECT FROM BULLIES.

26 THE GENIE IN DISNEY'S *ALADDIN* SAYS HE WILL GRANT ANY THREE WISHES ALADDIN WANTS.

27 IN *HARRY POTTER AND THE DEATHLY HALLOWS, PART 2*, HARRY LEARNS THAT SNAPE WAS A DEAR FRIEND OF HIS MOTHER.

28 IN *THE INCREDIBLE HULK*, DR. BRUCE BANNER MUST BE CAREFUL NOT TO GET TOO HUNGRY BECAUSE HE CAN QUICKLY TURN INTO A RAGING GREEN GIANT.

29 THE CLOWNFISH NEMO IN *FINDING NEMO* IS BORN IN A CORAL REEF OFF THE COAST OF HAWAII.

30 IN *HOW TO TRAIN YOUR DRAGON*, HICCUP MAKES FRIENDS WITH A DRAGON HE NAMES "GOBBER THE BELCH."

Star-STRUCK

TAYLOR SWIFT

1 What did pop star Taylor Swift do on her 18th birthday to show she was a good citizen?

a. registered to vote
b. released her album *Fearless*
c. won a Country Music Award
d. graduated from high school

2 Which of the following is true about singer Justin Bieber?

a. He has had more than 37 million followers on Twitter.
b. He was discovered on YouTube.
c. He is Canadian.
d. all of the above

3 **True or false?** Johnny Depp played the Mad Hatter in *Charlie and the Chocolate Factory*.

4 Which 2008 and 2012 Olympic star from Jamaica became the world's fastest sprinter?

a. Michael Phelps
b. Gabby Douglas
c. Usain Bolt
d. Peyton Manning

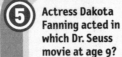

5 Actress Dakota Fanning acted in which Dr. Seuss movie at age 9?

a. *The Lorax*
b. *The Cat in the Hat*
c. *Oh, the Places You'll Go!*
d. *How the Grinch Stole Christmas*

6 Actress Maggie Smith plays which part in the *Harry Potter* movies?

a. Lily Potter
b. Sybil Trelawney
c. Minerva McGonagall
d. Dolores Umbridge

7 Which actress sings in the Disney Channel's *Camp Rock* movies?

a. Miley Cyrus
b. Avril Lavigne
c. Beyoncé
d. Demi Lovato

BRITISH ROYALS PRINCE WILLIAM AND CATHERINE, DUCHESS OF CAMBRIDGE

8 **True or false?** The U.S. Post Office printed pictures of Prince William and Kate Middleton on American postage stamps before their wedding in April 2011.

9 Which of the following is true about actress Emma Watson, who plays Hermione in the *Harry Potter* movies?

a. She has only acted in *Harry Potter* movies.
b. She has appeared in more than ten movies.
c. She was born in England.
d. She goes to college in France.

10 Which famous actress played a princess in *The Princess Diaries* and a queen in *Alice in Wonderland*?

a. Vanessa Hudgens
b. Emma Stone
c. Anne Hathaway
d. Keira Knightley

11 **True or false?** Actress Selena Gomez's first TV role was on *Barney & Friends*.

CHECK YOUR ANSWERS ON PAGES 161–162.

For Gamers Only!

1 What is the goal of the game *Bejeweled*?

a. to get a high score
b. to find the electric gem
c. to make a colorful picture
d. to be crowned with jewels

2 True or false? In *DragonVale*, water dragons walk well on land.

3 *Epic Mickey 2: The Power of Two* stars Mickey Mouse and what other character?

a. Donald Duck
b. Minnie Mouse
c. Oswald the Lucky Rabbit
d. Tweety Bird

4 True or false? Pigs were chosen as the target of attack in *Angry Birds* because so many people were getting sick from swine flu at the time the game was created.

5 In *Pokémon*, Keldeo is what kind of young animal?

a. kangaroo
b. horse
c. house cat
d. bear

6 In *Mario Kart*, what kind of transportation do the characters use?

a. karts and bikes
b. skis and snowboards
c. sleds and ice skates
d. inline skates and pogo sticks

7 In the gaming world, what is a *mod*?

a. a modern home
b. a model of the game
c. a device that loads the game
d. a modification players use to change a game

8 Where did the game *Yu-Gi-Oh!* come from?

a. Cambodia
b. China
c. Japan
d. Vietnam

9 How many people around the world are gamers and play at least an hour a day?

a. half a million
b. a million
c. half a billion
d. a billion

10 What does *Minecraft* commentator Jordan Maron call himself?

a. CaptainSparklez
b. Commander Sparks
c. Minecraft Maron
d. Crafty Jordan

11 In *Professor Layton and the Miracle Mask,* players must:

a. help Professor Layton get back home
b. solve puzzles
c. complete math problems
d. defeat the villain Bowser

12 Who is the main character in the game *The Legend of Zelda: The Wind Waker*?

a. Zelda
b. Link
c. Windy
d. Ganondorf

13 When was the first Nintendo gaming system created?

a. 1965
b. 1985
c. 1995
d. 2000

14 What is the most important thing to collect in the *Donkey Kong* Wii game *Country Returns*?

a. vines
b. barrels
c. bananas
d. coconuts

TETRIS

CHECK YOUR ANSWERS ON PAGES 161–162.

ULTIMATE POP CULTURE CHALLENGE

1 How old is the average video game player?
a. about 10 years old
b. about 18 years old
c. about 25 years old
d. about 30 years old

2 Which animals also appear in the game *Ant Smasher?*
a. cats
b. termites
c. bees
d. grasshoppers

3 Which elf does Orlando Bloom play in the movie *The Lord of the Rings: The Fellowship of the Ring?*
a. Galadriel
b. Celeborn
c. Legolas
d. Elrond

4 In the TV show *Good Luck Charlie*, who owns the business called Bob's Bugs Be Gone?
a. Charlie's dad
b. Charlie's uncle
c. Charlie's brothers
d. Charlie's grandfather

5 **TRUE OR FALSE?**
In the movie *Ratatouille*, Anton Ego is the evil chef at Gusteau's restaurant.

6 **TRUE OR FALSE?**
About half of the homes in the United States have a game console.

7 Jack Black was the voice of which character in the *Kung Fu Panda* movies?
a. Master Shifu
b. Tai Lung
c. Mr. Ping
d. Po

8 What is the name of SpongeBob's underwater town?
a. Bikini Bottom
b. Pineapple Grove
c. Aquarena Cantina
d. Coral Cove

9 TRUE OR FALSE?
More than half of YouTube's 800 million monthly visitors come from OUTSIDE of the United States.

10 Which of these athletes plays soccer?

a.

Eli Manning

b.

Serena Williams

c.

Michael Phelps

d.

Hope Solo

11 TRUE OR FALSE?
In the movie *Toy Story 3*, Andy's toys are sent to a school instead of his attic.

12 Elijah Wood, who plays Frodo Baggins in *The Lord of the Rings* movies, is also the voice of Mumble in which movie?
a. *Tron: Uprising*
b. *Happy Feet*
c. *American Dad!*
d. *The Legend of Spyro*

13 ULTIMATE BRAIN BUSTER

WHICH OF THESE VILLAINS IS NOT A MARVEL COMICS CHARACTER?

a.

The Thing

b.

Green Goblin

c.

Joker

d.

Red Skull

Get Back to NATURE

DO YOU THINK MY SMARTPHONE WILL WORK OUT HERE?

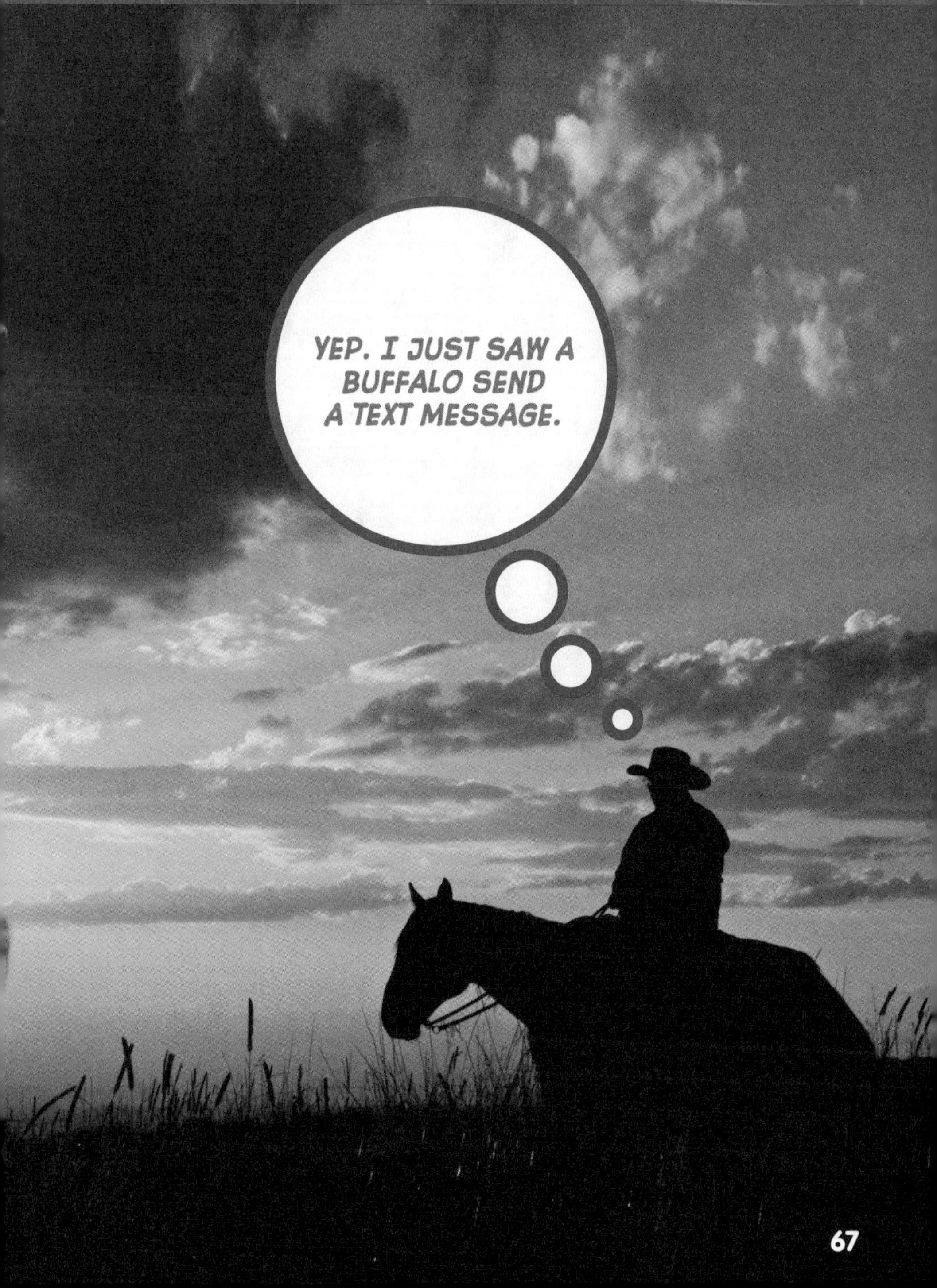
YEP. I JUST SAW A BUFFALO SEND A TEXT MESSAGE.

SURVIVAL GUIDE

1 You can survive without water for _____.

a. 3 to 5 days
b. 5 to 7 days
c. 10 days
d. 2 weeks

2 If you have water but no food, you can survive up to _____.

a. 3 days
b. 1 week
c. 3 weeks
d. 8 weeks

3 True or false? Grasshoppers will make a decent meal for a hungry person.

4 Which tool would be *most* useful if you were lost in the woods for a while?

a. an oven mitt
b. a water purifier
c. a comic book
d. toilet paper

5 True or false? If you have frostbitten toes, you should warm them by rubbing them.

6 What should you do if you get separated from your hiking buddies?

a. Stay put and signal for help.
b. Immediately set up a tent.
c. Do nothing.
d. Change into warmer clothes.

7 If you come across a bear in the woods, you should _____.

a. drop down to the ground
b. climb a tree
c. make lots of noise to scare it away
d. feed the bear

8 True or false? If you are stuck in the wilderness, you should never eat the bark of pine trees.

9 What should you do if you come across a swarm of wasps in the woods?

a. Run away fast.
b. Dig a hole in the ground.
c. Jump in a pond.
d. Hide in a tree.

10 True or false? A T-shirt is an excellent tool for catching fish.

12 Which of these ingredients should *not* be added to a cookout stew because it is poisonous?

a. fish
b. yew berry
c. grasshopper
d. grub

11 What is the best way to travel in the woods?

a. with a group
b. with no gear
c. during severe weather
d. in the middle of the night

13 Which edible water plant is known as the "supermarket of the swamp" because different parts of it can be eaten all year long?

a. cattail
b. lily pad
c. algae
d. watercress

14 Which household object could help you catch food if you were lost in the wilderness?

a. dental floss
b. a paper towel
c. shoe polish
d. a flashlight

It's a COOKOUT!

1 In what year were outdoor gas grills first sold for family use?
a. 1900
b. 1960
c. 1990
d. 2000

2 The shish kebab, a barbecue tradition whose name means "roast meat on a skewer," originally came from which country?
a. China
b. Russia
c. United States
d. Turkey

3 True or false? Ketchup can be used to clean copper pots and pans after a cookout.

4 About how many kernels are on a typical ear of corn?
a. 25
b. 100
c. 800
d. 50,000

5 How many pounds of marshmallows do Americans buy each year?
a. 15 million (6.8 million kg)
b. 30 million (13.6 million kg)
c. 60 million (27.2 million kg)
d. 90 million (40.8 million kg)

6 For how many years have humans likely been roasting meat on an open fire?
a. 400
b. 40,000
c. 400,000
d. 1.4 million

7 **True or false?** A dessert pie can't be made on the grill.

8 "Put another shrimp on the barbie, mate." What country has coin-operated barbecue grills along the beach?
a. Germany
b. Australia
c. U.S.A.
d. Israel

9 What is built into diners' tables at many Korean barbecue restaurants?
a. a sausage press
b. a ketchup maker
c. a barbecue grill
d. a mushroom garden

10 Which President hosted the first barbecue at the White House?
a. Jimmy Carter
b. Lyndon B. Johnson
c. Abraham Lincoln
d. William Taft

ANTS

11 Which cookout dish's name comes from a Dutch word meaning "cabbage salad"?
a. corn on the cob
b. hamburger
c. cole slaw
d. kebabs

12 **True or false?** Hot dogs are an approved food for U.S. astronauts to eat in space.

CHECK YOUR ANSWERS ON PAGES 163–164.

A STARRY SHOW

1 What causes the magnificent light show of the northern lights, also called the aurora borealis?

a. solar wind streams
b. exploding stars
c. black holes
d. solar eclipses

2 On what area of Earth's surface can you see the most stars in the sky?

a. suburban towns
b. big cities
c. large wilderness areas
d. any rooftop

3 Which planet is Earth's closest neighbor?

a. Mercury
b. Venus
c. Saturn
d. Neptune

4 Which is the last stage of the life cycle of most stars?

a. nebula
b. white dwarf
c. protostar
d. red giant

5 True or false? The same constellations are always seen in the sky from the same location.

6 When gazing at the night sky, what do people often mistake for stars?

a. helicopters
b. planets and satellites
c. asteroids and meteors
d. the moon

7 True or false? There is a constellation in the sky that looks like a hunter.

8 What causes the shadows and shapes we can see on a full moon?

a. weather on Earth
b. the man on the moon
c. cheese
d. craters

9 What tool do people use to get the best view of the moon and stars in the sky?

a. telescope
b. microscope
c. binoculars
d. glasses

10 True or False? Stars can be seen from Earth in the entire Northern Hemisphere every night of the year.

11 The millions of pieces of trash and debris floating around in Earth's atmosphere were caused by _____.

a. satellite explosions and collisions
b. astronaut garbage
c. launched space vehicles
d. all of the above

12 In 2004, scientists discovered a star made of _____.

a. gold
b. diamond
c. dust
d. salt

13 What object in the sky did sailors use to navigate ships?

a. clouds
b. the sun
c. the moon
d. constellations

14 On which planet is a day—the amount of time it takes for a planet to rotate on its axis—longer than 200 Earth days?

a. Venus
b. Mercury
c. Jupiter
d. Uranus

AURORA BOREALIS

MAP MANIA!
Wild Weather

1 EXTREME DRY WEATHER

How little rain falls every year in the Atacama Desert in Chile, one of the driest places on Earth?

a. .004 inches (.01 cm)
b. .5 inches (1.27 cm)
c. 1 inch (2.34 cm)
d. 2 inches (5 cm)

2 SANDSTORM

Sandstorms occur often in the Sahara desert when strong winds can blow a wall of sand and dust _____ high.

a. 20 feet (6 m)
b. 1 mile (1.6 km)
c. 10 miles (16 km)
d. 6 feet (1.8 m)

3 MONSOON

Changing ocean winds create monsoon seasons in southern Asia. What kind of weather can take place every day for months during this season?

a. fog
b. rain
c. tornadoes
d. snow

4 HEAT WAVE

In 2013, new colors had to be added to weather maps to show record-breaking temperatures in Australia. How hot did it get?

a. 90°F (32°C)
b. 110°F (43°C)
c. 200°F (93°C)
d. 129°F (54°C)

NORTH AMERICA
A
C
ATLANTIC OCEAN
PACIFIC OCEAN
SOUTH AMERICA
E

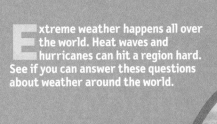

Extreme weather happens all over the world. Heat waves and hurricanes can hit a region hard. See if you can answer these questions about weather around the world.

ARCTIC OCEAN

EUROPE

ASIA

AFRICA

D

B

PACIFIC OCEAN

INDIAN OCEAN

AUSTRALIA

F

ANTARCTICA

5 HURRICANE

How many inches of rain did Hurricane Sandy dump over the Atlantic Coast region of the U.S. in October 2012?

a. 30 inches (76 cm)
b. 18 inches (46 cm)
c. 7 inches (18 cm)
d. 3 inches (8 cm)

6 TORNADO

How many tornadoes occurred over a four-day period in Tornado Alley, in the United States in April 2011—setting a new record?

a. 26
b. 53
c. 120

7-12 MATCH EACH

HIGHLIGHTED AREA ON THE MAP WITH THE LOCATIONS MENTIONED IN THE QUESTIONS ABOVE.

CHECK YOUR ANSWERS ON PAGES 163–164.

Amazing ANTARCTICA

ICE FLOE

1 How much of Antarctica is covered in ice?

a. 25% c. 83%
b. 49% d. 98%

SCOTT BASE
SCIENTIFIC CAMP

2 Most people living in Antarctica are scientific researchers. How many people make up the summertime population?

a. 400
b. 4,000
c. 40,000
d. 400,000

3 True or false? Antarctica is the windiest place on the planet.

4 Which geographical landmark is located in Antarctica?

a. North Pole
b. South Pole
c. Grand Canyon
d. Mariana Trench

5 The sun never rises in Antarctica during which month of the year?

a. January
b. June
c. March
d. October

6 True or false? There are 12 countries on the continent of Antarctica.

ICEBERG OFF THE COAST
OF ANTARCTICA

7 The first successful expedition to the Antarctic took place in the _____.

a. 1540s
b. 1680s
c. 1820s
d. 1930s

EMPEROR PENGUIN

8 Which word *best* describes Antarctica?

a. forest
b. desert
c. valley
d. ocean

9 If all of the ice in Antarctica melted, the world's oceans would rise by _____.

a. 49 feet (15 m)
b. 98 feet (30 m)
c. 200 feet (61 m)
d. 394 feet (120 m)

PALM WEEVIL SNOUT BEETLE

10 **True or false?** There are no insects in Antarctica.

11 What does the emperor penguin of Antarctica eat?

a. crabs
b. seals
c. lobster
d. tiny shrimp-like animals called krill

12 What is the average summer temperature in Antarctica?

a. 20°F (−6.7°C)
b. 40°F (4.4°C)
c. 50°F (10°C)
d. 70°F (21.1°C)

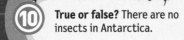

CHECK YOUR ANSWERS ON PAGES 163–164.

Out at Sea

1. THE COLOSSAL SQUID, THE WORLD'S LARGEST SQUID, IS LONGER THAN A SCHOOL BUS.

2. HUMANS HAVE EXPLORED MORE THAN 90 PERCENT OF THE WORLD'S OCEANS.

3. AN OCTOPUS HAS FOUR HEARTS.

4. A BLUE WHALE'S HEART IS ABOUT THE SIZE OF A HOUSE.

5. ORCAS, ALSO CALLED KILLER WHALES, BELONG TO THE DOLPHIN FAMILY.

6. THE WATER PRESSURE IN THE DEEPEST PART OF THE WORLD'S OCEANS IS EQUIVALENT TO THE WEIGHT OF 50 JET PLANES ON THE SHOULDERS OF ONE PERSON.

7. THE ATLANTIC OCEAN IS THE WORLD'S LARGEST OCEAN.

8. ONE-FOURTH OF THE WORLD'S POPULATION RELIES ON THE OCEANS FOR ITS MAIN SOURCE OF PROTEIN.

9. THE FASTEST SHARK IS THE MAKO.

10. THE WORLD'S LONGEST MOUNTAIN RANGE LIES ON THE OCEAN FLOOR.

11. A TABLESPOON OF SEAWATER CONTAINS ONLY A FEW ORGANISMS OR BACTERIA.

12. SOUND TRAVELS MORE SLOWLY THROUGH WATER THAN IT DOES THROUGH AIR.

13. THERE'S GOLD TO BE FOUND IN THE OCEAN.

14. AT LEAST ONE CREATURE LIVING IN THE SEA HAS BLUE BLOOD.

15. ABOUT 40 PERCENT OF EARTH'S VOLCANIC ACTIVITY HAPPENS IN THE OCEANS.

16 SCIENTISTS CURRENTLY HAVE NAMED ABOUT 200,000 MARINE SPECIES.

17 MOST OF THE OCEAN'S HEAT IS IN THE TOP 10 FEET (3 M) OF WATER.

18 EARTHQUAKES UNDER THE SEA CAN CAUSE HURRICANES TO FORM.

19 THE LEVELS OF OCEAN WATER HAVE BEEN RISING FOR MORE THAN A CENTURY.

20 THE ATLANTIC OCEAN GETS ITS NAME FROM AN ANCIENT GREEK MYTH.

21 THE FIRST PERSON TO DIVE INTO THE OCEAN WITHOUT BREATHING DOVE 344 FEET (105 M).

22 THERE ARE ABOUT 25,000 ISLANDS IN THE PACIFIC OCEAN.

23 MORE OIL IS DRILLED IN THE MEDITERRANEAN SEA THAN ANYWHERE ELSE ON EARTH.

24 BLUE WHALES LIVING IN THE OCEANS TODAY ARE LARGER THAN ANY DINOSAUR KNOWN TO HAVE LIVED.

25 THE GRAY WHALE MIGRATES 10,000 MILES (16,100 KM) EACH YEAR.

26 THE OCEANS' TIDES ARE AFFECTED BY THE GRAVITATIONAL PULL BETWEEN EARTH AND THE MOON.

27 SCIENTISTS ARE LOOKING FOR ORGANISMS ON THE OCEAN FLOOR TO MAKE INTO CANCER MEDICINE.

28 THE WORD *SCUBA* COMES FROM THE PHRASE "SOLO CONTINUOUS UNDERSEA BATHING APPARATUS."

29 DURING THE SUMMER, THE ARCTIC OCEAN IS ALMOST TOTALLY COVERED BY ICE.

30 CORAL IS SO SIMILAR TO HUMAN BONE THAT DOCTORS HAVE USED IT IN OPERATIONS TO REPAIR BONES.

CHECK YOUR ANSWERS ON PAGES 163–164.

A DISTINCT DESERT

1 Which of these living things is found only in the Sonoran Desert, which stretches across parts of the southwestern United States and northwest Mexico?

a. saguaro cactus
b. jackrabbit
c. monitor lizard
d. desert bloodwood tree

2 True or false? A person bitten by a desert rattlesnake will need about 20 vials of antivenom, or venom antidote.

3 The Sonoran Desert covers how much land?

a. 10,000 square miles (26,000 km²)
b. 42,000 square miles (109,000 km²)
c. 100,000 square miles (259,000 km²)
d. 54,000 square miles (140,000 km²)

4 True or false? The creosote bush of the Sonoran Desert tastes really bad.

5 One desert plant, called the creosote bush, is one of the _____ plants in the world.

a. oldest
b. prickliest
c. smelliest
d. smallest

6 The saguaro cactus flower is the state flower of which southwestern state in the United States?

a. Oklahoma
b. California
c. Arizona
d. Texas

7 How does the desert wren use the cactus to stay alive?

a. It hangs its food on the cactus's spines.
b. It lives inside the trunk of the cactus.
c. It sits on top of the cactus to watch for prey.
d. It lays its eggs in the roots of the cactus.

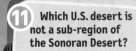

Get Back to NATURE

8 How much rain can an area get per year in order to be called a desert?
- **a.** less than 1 inch (2.5 cm)
- **b.** less than 10 inches (25 cm)
- **c.** less than 20 inches (50 cm)
- **d.** less than 50 inches (127 cm)

9 How much of Earth's land surface is covered by desert?
- **a.** one-fifth
- **b.** one-fourth
- **c.** one-third
- **d.** one-half

10 **True or false?** About 2,500 different kinds of edible plants grow in the Sonoran Desert.

11 Which U.S. desert is not a sub-region of the Sonoran Desert?
- **a.** Yuma Desert
- **b.** Colorado Desert
- **c.** Mojave Desert
- **d.** Tonopah Desert

12 **True or false?** Summertime temperatures at the southern part of the Sonoran Desert can reach 134°F (57°C) in the shade.

13 How long do saguaro cacti, which are native to the Sonoran Desert, typically live?
- **a.** 40–50 years
- **b.** 80–120 years
- **c.** 150–200 years
- **d.** 300–350 years

SAGUARO CACTUS IN THE SONORAN DESERT

14 The gila monster is the _____ lizard in the United States.
- **a.** fastest
- **b.** largest
- **c.** smallest
- **d.** deadliest

ULTIMATE NATURE CHALLENGE

1 Early Americans cooked baked beans outdoors with
_____.

a. maple syrup and bear fat
b. molasses and sugar
c. pork fat and cinnamon
d. bacon and orange juice

2 How much water should you bring into the desert for one day if little physical activity is planned?

a. none
b. a half gallon (1.9 L)
c. 1 gallon (3.8 L)
d. 5 gallons (19 L)

3 TRUE OR FALSE?
The Big Dipper constellation is made of seven stars.

4 Which planet can't be seen from Earth without using a telescope or binoculars?

a. Uranus
b. Mercury
c. Venus
d. Mars

5 The amount of frozen water on Antarctica is equal to the amount of liquid water in the _____.

a. Bering Strait
b. Atlantic Ocean
c. Pacific Ocean
d. Mediterranean Sea

6 TRUE OR FALSE?
A possible name for the first tropical storm of a season is *Benito*.

7 How much time passes between one high tide in the ocean and the next?

a. 2 hours
b. 7 hours
c. 12 hours
d. 24 hours

Get Back to NATURE

 Which animal does *not* live in a desert?

a.
rattlesnake

b.
gila monster

c.
roadrunner

d.
macaw

 Which outdoor adventure has the biggest risk of avalanches?
a. climbing Mount Everest
b. visiting the South Pole
c. visiting the North Pole
d. hiking in the Gobi Desert

10
TRUE OR FALSE?
The sun is the star closest to Earth.

 Which living thing is called "the ship of the desert"?
a. saguaro cactus
b. antelope
c. fox
d. camel

 How tall were the waves of the largest tsunami ever recorded in 1737?
a. 178 feet (54 m)
b. 210 feet (64 m)
c. 385 feet (117 m)
d. 433 feet (132 m)

 ULTIMATE BRAIN BUSTER

WHAT UNUSUAL ANIMAL APPEARS IN THIS PHOTOGRAPH?
a. jellyfish
b. giant octopus
c. colossal squid
d. baleen whale

Blast FROM THE PAST

AFTER WE GET GLASS FOR THE WINDOWS.

FLASHback!

1 In 1996, which Japanese collection of video games, cards, and anime made Ash and Pikachu world famous?

a. Pokémon
b. My Neighbor Totoro
c. Dragonball
d. Minecraft

2 **True or false?** The smiley face was first drawn in 1963 to make people happy.

3 *Paku-paku*, the Japanese sound for "munch," gave this classic video game from 1980 its name.

a. *Centipede*
b. *Donkey Kong*
c. *Pac-Man*
d. *Super Mario Bros*

4 By the end of 1983, 3 million of these dolls had been "adopted."

a. Barbie
b. Cabbage Patch Kids
c. Tickle Me Elmo
d. Transformers

5 How much did the first handheld mobile phone weigh?

a. half a pound (.23 kg)
b. 2.5 pounds (1.1 kg)
c. 5 pounds (2.3 kg)
d. 100 pounds (45.4 kg)

6 Which group of video games for kids is the most successful ever?

a. Mario series
b. Batman series
c. DuckTales series
d. Space Invaders series

7 If you were doing the "Macarena" at a party in the 1990s, you were _____.

a. skateboarding
b. dancing
c. eating cookies
d. standing on your head

PEZ CANDY DISPENSERS

8 True or false? The candy PEZ got its name in 1927 from the German word for peppermint, *pfefferminz.*

9 People say the Frisbee was named after _____.

a. a pie pan from the Frisbie Pie Company
b. a frizzy hair style
c. an alien spacecraft from the planet "Frzz"
d. a swarm of bees

10 *American Idol*'s Ryan Seacrest was inspired by Dick Clark and his show _____.

a. *The Ed Sullivan Show*
b. *American Bandstand*
c. *Wheel of Fortune*
d. *To Tell the Truth*

11 This toy has been around for more than 2,000 years. Today, people use it to "walk the dog" and "rock the baby."

a. a jump rope
b. a harmonica
c. a yo-yo
d. a skateboard

12 In the 1980s, what fashion trend kept girls both warm and "cool" in exercise class?

a. sandals
b. Hello Kitty backpacks
c. miniskirts
d. leg warmers

14 True or false? LEGO bricks have been around for more than 500 years.

13 Which of these toys is more than 50 years old?

a. ant farms
b. Play-Doh
c. Etch A Sketch
d. all of the above

CHECK YOUR ANSWERS ON PAGES 164–165.

IN KNIGHTLY FASHION

1 Armored clothing, called chain mail, was made of connecting metal _____.
a. animals
b. rings
c. nails
d. shells

2 Plate armor, the heavy covering that protected a knight's body, was made of what material?
a. wood
b. iron or steel
c. dinner plates
d. hard leather

3 When did knights wear armor?
a. for parades
b. for competitions
c. for combat
d. all of the above

4 What was a *coat of arms* in the Middle Ages?
a. a symbol that identified the knight
b. a coat made out of octopus
c. a colored feather on a helmet
d. a heavy leather jacket

5 True or false? Combat armor was generally the lightest kind of armor.

6 How was a lance used?
a. to help mount a horse
b. as a walking stick
c. as a jousting weapon
d. as a parade flag

7 True or false? In the Middle Ages, knights in armor were too heavy to actually ride on horses, so knights just posed for pictures on horses.

8 True or false? Women were forbidden to fight in battles.

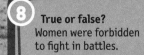

9 What did a jousting helmet always have?

a. built-in sunglasses
b. narrow eye slits
c. a megaphone
d. a wig attached

10 When a knight threw down his gauntlet, another word for a glove, what was he accepting?

a. an invitation to dinner
b. a kiss from a lady
c. a challenge to fight
d. a call from his mother

11 What was a knight's shield made of?

a. porcupine quills
b. wood and metal
c. bubble wrap
d. carved stone

12 What helped a knight in armor climb up on a horse?

a. stirrups
b. stairs
c. a dragon
d. a ladder

13 Warriors eventually stopped wearing metal armor because it couldn't protect them from which "new" weapon?

a. a sword
b. lawn darts
c. a bow and arrow
d. a gun

CHECK YOUR ANSWERS ON PAGES 164–165.

ROCK ON!

1 What musical group is considered by some people as the most famous British rock band of all time?

a. The Monkees
b. Herman's Hermits
c. The Beatles
d. Led Zeppelin

THE FAB FOUR

ELVIS PRESLEY

2 What song did Elvis Presley sing to a Basset Hound on a television show in 1956?

a. "Hound Dog"
b. "Rock Around the Clock"
c. "Jailhouse Rock"
d. "A Big Hunk O' Love"

3 Which Korean music video was the most popular music video of 2012 and sparked a new dance craze?

a. "Ho Hey"
b. "Gangnam Style"
c. "Thriller"
d. "Yellow Submarine"

STEVIE WONDER

4 American musician Stevie Wonder became blind at a young age, but he learned to play many instruments, including the ____.

a. vuvuzela
b. kazoo
c. piano
d. accordion

5 Sparkly, mirrored balls, often seen hanging in 1970s dance clubs, were named after which dance craze?

a. waltz
b. punk
c. hip hop
d. disco

6 The hairstyle shown in the picture at right was popular at punk rock concerts in the 1970s. What is it called?

a. mullet
b. mohawk
c. beehive
d. bob

7 True or false? Beyoncé is a guitar player in a rock band called Kiss.

8 In the 1980s, American performer Madonna was best known for ____.

a. writing stories about the Beatles
b. yodeling in the Alps
c. waltzing with the Swedish group ABBA
d. singing pop music

9 Say "Graahar!" What flesh-eating monsters do you see in Michael Jackson's famous 1980s music video "Thriller"?

a. vampires
b. zombies
c. werewolves
d. square dancers

MICHAEL JACKSON

10 True or false? Over 30 years ago, MTV played only music videos.

11 Which of these popular singers grew up on an island in the Caribbean in the 1990s?

a. Rihanna
b. Paul McCartney
c. Justin Bieber
d. Mozart

12 The Beach Boys caught a wave of popularity in the 1960s with a song about surfing and girls in which U.S. state?

a. Alaska
b. Texas
c. Oklahoma
d. California

SURFERS

13 People liked to "swing" to the trumpet playing of American musician Louis Armstrong in the 1950s. For what kind of music was he known?

a. playground music
b. circus music
c. jazz
d. heavy metal

14 Folk music fans loved American musician Bob Dylan. Why did folk fans "booo" him at a 1965 concert?

a. Giant fans blew air on the crowd.
b. He switched from an acoustic guitar to an electric guitar.
c. He wore a ghost costume.
d. He performed a tap dance...badly.

BOB DYLAN

CHECK YOUR ANSWERS ON PAGES 164–165.

National Parks ROAD TRIP!

GREET SMOKY MOUNTAINS

(1) Which national park is the most visited park in the United States?

a. Yosemite (California)
b. Yellowstone (Wyoming)
c. Grand Canyon (Arizona)
d. Great Smoky Mountains (from North Carolina to Tennessee)

(2) True or false? Banff National Park in Alberta, Canada, was established in 1885 to protect Canada's maple trees and maple syrup businesses.

(3) True or false? Yellowstone's famous geyser "Old Faithful" was named in 1870 after a grizzly bear that showed up every morning to shower in its waters.

OLD FAITHFUL

(4) India's Kanha National Park, famous for its tigers, was the inspiration for which classic children's book?

a. *Winnie-the-Pooh*
b. *Charlotte's Web*
c. *The Jungle Book*
d. *The Story of Doctor Dolittle*

(5) The Lakota people called this South Dakota park "land bad" long ago because there is little water and the land is rugged.

a. Badlands
b. Devil's Tower
c. Wind Cave
d. Mount Rushmore

TIGER

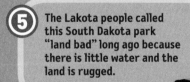

BADLANDS

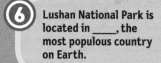
6 Lushan National Park is located in ____, the most populous country on Earth.

a. Mexico
b. Russia
c. China
d. New York

SEQUOIA TREE

GENERAL SHERMAN

7 In which California park can you find a famous 2,300-2,700-year-old sequoia tree?

a. Sequoia National Park
b. Sea World
c. Disneyland
d. Joshua Tree

8 Human footprints from more than three million years ago were found in which national park?

a. Serengeti (African plains of Tanzania)
b. Bandipur (southern India)
c. Hustai (steppe of Mongolia)
d. Amazonia in Brazil (South America)

9 **True or false?** A park in Alberta, Canada, is on land where dinosaurs walked around about 75 million years ago.

CLIFF PALACE

10 For more than 700 years, Pueblo Indians lived in homes built into the cliffs of what is now part of which national park?

a. Mesa Verde (Colorado)
b. Volcanoes National Park (Hawaii)
c. Big Bend (Texas)
d. Carlsbad Caverns (New Mexico)

11 **True or false?** In the early 1920s, a visitor could ride into the Bat Cave at Carlsbad Caverns in a big bucket also used to gather bat guano ("droppings").

Eat, Drink, and Be MERRY!

1 Which famous TV show for little kids takes its name from one of the oldest edible seeds in history?

a. *Poppy Cat*
b. *Sesame Street*
c. *SpongeBob SquarePants*
d. *Blue's Clues*

2 Why did ancient Egyptians pickle certain foods?

a. to eat them with hot dogs
b. to soften them
c. to color them
d. to preserve them

3 True or false? Ancient Greeks used dill and other common herbs to heal the body.

4 What did the Spanish explorers take from Mexico's Aztec Indians and use to make hot chocolate?

a. vanilla and cocoa beans
b. coffee beans
c. gold coins
d. chili powder

5 True or false? In the mid-1800s, a lollipop was a hard candy without a stick.

6 The vitamin C from which fruit helped prevent sailors from getting scurvy, a disease that causes sores and rotting gums?

a. watermelon
b. lemon
c. papaya
d. plum

7 What **nickname** did Dutch Pilgrims use for doughnuts?

a. oily cakes
b. fried goodness
c. sweet wheels
d. fat rings

8 Which substance, similar to a food seasoning, was used to preserve mummies?

a. sugar
b. cheesy garlic powder
c. vinegar
d. salt

9 True or false? Honey, the oldest sweetener on Earth, was once used as money.

10 How did American astronaut John Glenn eat food on his first trip into space in 1961?

a. with a spoon
b. in dried chunks
c. on a plate
d. from a squeeze tube

11 Spanish explorers brought this citrus fruit with them to the New World and then planted it in **Florida**, where it grows today!

a. apple
b. orange
c. grapefruit
d. strawberry

12 What snack food became popular after people tried it at a baseball stadium in the **1970s**?

a. popcorn
b. nachos
c. fried bananas
d. peanut-butter-and-jelly sandwiches

13 Where does the saying "**Eat, drink, and be merry**" come from?

a. Shakespeare
b. the Bible
c. medieval banquets
d. *Harry Potter and the Sorcerer's Stone*

DragonVille

1 The Chinese dragon is an ancient symbol of what?

a. goodness
b. evil
c. wealth
d. power

2 In the stories of *My Father's Dragon*, Elmer's baby dragon loves to eat which stinky food?

a. skunk cabbage
b. cat food
c. brussels sprouts
d. cotton candy

3 What real-life dragon is actually a 300-pound lizard that was discovered by Europeans 100 years ago?

a. Leafy seadragon
b. Norwegian ridgeback
c. Komodo dragon
d. Charley horse

4 In which popular story is Bastian Bux rescued by the luckdragon?

a. *Beauty and the Beast*
b. *The Neverending Story*
c. *Captain America*
d. *E.T. the Extra-Terrestrial*

5 What popular song for little kids mentions dragons "in a land called Honah Lee"?

a. "Ride the Dragon"
b. "Puff, the Magic Dragon"
c. "Little Red Dragon"
d. "Norbert's Song"

6 This 1998 animated movie follows the adventures of a brave girl and her dragon Mushu during China's great Han Dynasty.

a. *Spirited Away*
b. *Brave*
c. *Mulan*
d. *Eragon*

7 True or false? To frighten enemies, Vikings placed big carved dragon heads on the front of their ships.

8 In what country do people call themselves "Descendants of the Dragon"?

a. United States   c. Germany
b. Canada   d. China

9 This app allows you to raise and care for your own dragons.

a. DragonVale   c. DragonPark
b. DragonHatch   d. DragonTales

10 At the end of the 1959 Disney movie *Sleeping Beauty*, who turns into a dragon?

a. Prince Phillip
b. King Stefan
c. the villain Maleficent
d. Snow White

11 True or false? The famous line, "Never laugh at live dragons, Bilbo you fool!" comes from the classic tale *Charlotte's Web*.

12 In a popular book by Christopher Paolini, which teen boy is friends with a dragon named Saphira?

a. Harry Potter   c. Percy Jackson
b. Eragon   d. Elmer

13 True or false? Barney is a fierce black dragon who is the star of a children's TV show.

Famous FICTION

1. **The Phantom Tollbooth** is about a boy who drives through a magic tollbooth and ____.
   - a. has adventures
   - b. wins a pot of gold
   - c. becomes a wizard
   - d. gets invisible teeth

2. Omri's life turns upside down in this book when an Iroquois warrior from the 1700s comes alive in his room.
   - a. *The Indian in the Cupboard*
   - b. *Johnny Tremain*
   - c. *The Arrow Over the Door*
   - d. *Sing Down the Moon*

3. In *The Lightning Thief*, Percy Jackson is a modern boy who is forced to learn a lot about ____.
   - a. European history
   - b. the Chinese language
   - c. Greek mythology
   - d. classical music

4. In which book does a clever spider write the words "Some Pig," saving her best friend from slaughter?
   - a. *The Secret Garden*
   - b. *Charlotte's Web*
   - c. *The BFG*
   - d. *Shiloh*

5. **True or false?** Long before he wrote the book *Stuart Little*, author E.B. White dreamed about a boy who was as tiny as a mouse!

STUART LITTLE

6 Heroes Stanley Yelnats and Zero Zeroni dig all day long in what famous story?
a. *Holes*
b. *Captain Underpants*
c. *I, Amber Brown*
d. *Frindle*

7 In the King Arthur stories, why did the king want his knights to sit at a round table?
a. so everyone could reach the food
b. so there was no "head of the table," which made the knights feel like equals
c. so the table was easy to roll when it had to be moved
d. both a and c

8 Peter, Susan, Edmund, and Lucy find a magic closet in what story?
a. *A Wrinkle in Time*
b. *Hatchet*
c. *Shiloh*
d. *The Lion, the Witch and the Wardrobe*

9 Author Laura Ingalls Wilder writes about her life in a pioneer family in which novel?
a. *Little House in the Big Woods*
b. *Little House on the Prairie*
c. *On the Banks of Plum Creek*
d. all of the above

10 **True or false?** Some of the *American Girl* books tell stories of characters who live at various times in American history.

11 *Ella Enchanted* is the story of Ella, who has to live with a wicked step-mother and stepsisters. What classic story does it resemble?
a. "Cinderella"
b. "Hansel and Gretel"
c. "The Little Mermaid"
d. "Snow White and the Seven Dwarfs"

12 **True or false?** *Esperanza Rising* is the story of a Mexican family that struggles to survive once they move to the United States.

13 *Tales of a Fourth Grade Nothing* was the first "Fudge" book written by which famous author?
a. Shel Silverstein
b. Judy Blume
c. Paula Danziger
d. Roald Dahl

ANIMALS TAMED by TIME

1 True or false? If a person had shaved eyebrows in ancient Egypt, it might mean that the family cat had died.

2 How long have dogs been kept as pets?

a. more than 100 years
b. more than 1,000 years
c. more than 10,000 years
d. none of the above

3 True or false? A *domesticated* animal belongs to a species that has changed over generations, learning to work with people.

4 Which animals often pulled early American farm plows?

a. sled dogs
b. oxen
c. donkeys
d. elephants

5 Sheep were one of the first animals to be raised for their ____.

a. meat
b. fleece
c. milk
d. all of the above

6 For 5,000 years, people have used the cocoon of this wiggly creature to weave beautiful silk!

a. silkworm
b. butterfly
c. spider
d. cockroach

7 Farmers began to raise this big, flightless bird for its feathers in the 1800s.

a. owl
b. eagle
c. penguin
d. ostrich

8 Which animals were the first to become farm animals about 10,000 years ago?

a. sheep and goats
b. cows
c. turkeys and chickens
d. pigs

9 Farmers have kept track of **wandering** cows since the 1400s by using what?

a. ear tags
b. cowbells
c. GPS
d. nose rings

10 True or false? Today, the term horsepower explains the power of a car, but in the 1780s it was used to describe the strength of children.

11 "It's **raining** cats and dogs" is a saying from the 1500s. What does it mean?

a. There's trouble ahead.
b. Be grateful.
c. It's raining hard.
d. The roof is leaking.

12 Four thousand years ago, before the time of dairy cows, butter was made from the **milk** of _____.

a. sheep
b. yaks
c. goats
d. all of the above

13 Why did Spanish explorers bring **pigs** on their voyages in the 1500s?

a. Pigs could be eaten for food.
b. Pigs needed little care.
c. Pigs could squeal if enemies approached.
d. a and b

14 Three million years ago, this cousin to the camel moved from North America to South America.

a. llama
b. giraffe
c. snow leopard
d. sheep dog

MAP MANIA!
WORLD TRAVELERS

1 MARCO POLO

On his journey to what land did Marco Polo learn about paper money?
a. Italy
b. China
c. Japan
d. Africa

2 HERNANDO DE SOTO

Spaniard Hernando de Soto explored this mighty North American river (below) 343 years before author Mark Twain wrote about Huck Finn's adventures there!
a. Nile River
b. Colorado River
c. Missouri River
d. Mississippi River

3 CORONADO

Spanish conqueror Francisco Vasquez de Coronado found which of these beautiful places in the southwestern United States?
a. Grand Canyon
b. Zuni pueblos
c. Colorado River
d. all of the above

NORTH AMERICA

F

E

ATLANTIC OCEAN

PACIFIC OCEAN

SOUTH AMERICA

A

H istory is filled with explorers who journeyed to exciting lands. Answer these questions, then match each explorer to the place on the map where he made a discovery.

4 VASCO DA GAMA

Portuguese explorer Vasco da Gama wanted to find a direct route to what Asian country to get pepper and other spices?

a. America
b. England
c. India
d. Australia

ARCTIC OCEAN
EUROPE
ASIA
AFRICA
D
C
B
PACIFIC OCEAN
INDIAN OCEAN
AUSTRALIA
ANTARCTICA

5 HOWARD CARTER

In 1922, British archaeologist Howard Carter discovered the tomb of which Egyptian pharaoh, shown here?

a. King Lear
b. King Ramses II
c. King Tut
d. King Kong

6 FERDINAND MAGELLAN

True or false?
Ferdinand Magellan proved Earth was round by being the first explorer to find a sea route around South America.

SOUTHERNMOST TIP OF SOUTH AMERICA

7–12 THE HIGHLIGHTED AREAS IN ORANGE ON

THE MAP MARK WHERE EACH TRAVELER EXPLORED AND MADE A DISCOVERY. MATCH EACH TRAVELER TO THE PLACE OF HIS IMPORTANT DISCOVERY.

GAME SHOW
ULTIMATE
BLAST FROM THE PAST CHALLENGE

1 Between 1927 and 1941, skilled blasters used dynamite to carve Mount Rushmore in which mountains in South Dakota, U.S.A.?

a. The Alps
b. Ozark Mountains
c. Andes Mountains
d. Black Hills

2 TRUE OR FALSE? The Hoover Dam, which spans part of the Colorado River between Arizona and Nevada, U.S.A., is more than 150 feet (46 m) taller than the Washington Monument in Washington, D.C., U.S.A.

3 Which character hung out with a band of outlaws in England's Sherwood Forest?

a. Robin Hood
b. Iron Man
c. Gandalf
d. Harry Potter

4 A dragon from the Viking era appears with Hiccup in what popular movie?

a. *How to Train Your Dragon*
b. *Sleeping Beauty*
c. *Kung Fu Panda*
d. *Pete's Dragon*

5 In 1984, the Statue of Liberty's torch was repaired and coated with _____ to make it shine super bright.

a. diamonds
b. thin sheets of gold
c. yellow paint
d. lasers

6 TRUE OR FALSE?

Women were the first to compete at the start of the Olympic Games in 776 BCE.

7 Who put pictures of chickens on royal tombs and built incubators to hatch eggs more than 2,000 years ago?

a. British   c. Chinese
b. Aztecs   d. Egyptians

8 Bach, Beethoven, and Mozart were all famous _____.

a. singers
b. dancers
c. composers
d. drummers

9 **TRUE OR FALSE?** In their TV show from the 1990s, the Power Rangers were teenagers who sometimes used "dragon power" to fight evil.

10 *The Hobbit*'s Bilbo Baggins wore a coat of Mithril, a metal found in Middle-earth that was _____ than steel.

a. stronger
b. shinier
c. lighter
d. all of the above

11 Which dog from a classic movie was in real life a mixed breed found at an animal shelter?

a.
Lassie

c.
Toto

b.
Benji

d.
Beethoven

12 **TRUE OR FALSE?** A computer program named Chinook became the world champion of checkers in 1994.

13 Where does the story of *Anne of Green Gables* take place?

a. Waikiki, Hawaii
b. Galveston, Texas
c. Prince Edward Island, Canada
d. Green Island, England

14 The Aztec Indians popped these kernels way back in the 1500s for food and decorations.

a. pepper
b. corn
c. barley
d. pop rocks

15 Table tennis, or Ping-Pong, originated in which merry old country in the 1880s?

a. China
b. Japan
c. United States
d. England

16 **ULTIMATE BRAIN BUSTER**

WHICH ADVENTURER SHOWN IN THIS PICTURE BECAME THE FIRST WOMAN TO TRAVEL INTO SPACE?

a. Hermione Granger
b. Valentina Tereshkova
c. Sally Ride
d. Kate Middleton

CHECK YOUR ANSWERS ON PAGES 164–165.

It All ADDS UP!

I JUST CAN'T SEEM TO FALL ASLEEP AT NIGHT.

Count Your Critters

1 How many muscles are in a cat's ear?
a. 3
b. 14
c. 32
d. 42

2 About how many different kinds of dog breeds are there?
a. 250
b. 400
c. 800
d. 2,000

3 A group of chickens is called a flock. What is a group of peacocks called?
a. a muster
b. a clutch
c. a gaggle
d. a herd

4 It is estimated that in one acre (.4 hectares) of woodland, spiders can eat more than ___ pounds of insects per year.
a. 8
b. 18
c. 80
d. 8,000

5 **True or false?** There are 1,000 living species in the canine family.

PEACOCK

6 What is the top speed of an American quarter horse?
a. 15 mph (24 kph)
b. 25 mph (40 kph)
c. 50 mph (80 kph)
d. 75 mph (121 kph)

AMERICAN QUARTER HORSE

7 The oldest skunk fossil ever found is ___ years old.
a. 11 million
b. 5 million
c. 1 million
d. 500,000

8 Thumbelina holds the Guinness record for smallest miniature horse at ___ tall.
a. 4 inches (10 cm)
b. 17 inches (43 cm)
c. 34.5 inches (88 cm)
d. 5 feet (1.5 m)

9 The longest Burmese python was found in Florida's Everglades in 2012. How long was it?
a. 8.3 feet (2.5 m)
b. 12.2 feet (3.7 m)
c. 17.7 feet (5.4 m)
d. 23.6 feet (7.2 m)

HEDGEHOG

10 One prickly animal, the adult hedgehog, has about how many spines?
a. 200–400
b. 500–1,000
c. 2,000–3,000
d. 5,000–7,000

11 How long can a pet goldfish live?
a. 1 year
b. 5 years
c. 25 years
d. 80 years

12 True or false? Parrots have four toes on each foot.

GOLDFISH

CHECK YOUR ANSWERS ON PAGES 166–167.

Treasure Chest

1 Two Englishmen recently discovered a treasure of **50,000** coins from 2,000 years ago. How much are the coins worth today?

a. $1 million   c. $10 million
b. $5 million   d. $15 million

2 When the *Titanic* sank in 1912, a shipment of diamonds worth ____ in today's money went down with the ship and has never been found.

a. $1 million   c. $900 million
b. $300 million   d. $100 billion

3 The "Pearl of Allah," the world's largest pearl, is about the size of a bowling ball and worth about **$60 million.** How much does it weigh?

a. 6 pounds (2.7 kg)   c. 11 pounds (5 kg)
b. 8 pounds (3.6 kg)   d. 14 pounds (6.4 kg)

4 The world's largest diamond on record weighs 545.67 carats, which is about _____.

a. 2 ounces (57 g)   c. 5 pounds (2 kg)
b. ¼ pound (113 g)   d. 167 pounds (75 kg)

6 Much of the United States' gold reserves are stored in a vault in **Fort Knox**, Kentucky. How much is the gold worth at today's prices?

a. $3.5 million   c. $1.2 billion
b. $558 million   d. $208 billion

5 How much would **$1 million dollars** weigh if you used only **$100 bills?**

a. 20 pounds (9 kg)
b. 50 pounds (23 kg)
c. 180 pounds (82 kg)
d. 470 pounds (213 kg)

7 True or false? In 2011, French police found jewels worth $25 million hidden in a sewer in Paris.

8 At 57,500 carats, one of the world's largest emeralds was unearthed in **Brazil** and is about the size of a ____.

a. green pea
b. soccer ball
c. watermelon
d. truck

9 How often can the United States secretary of the treasury change the design of coins?

a. every 5 years
b. every 10 years
c. every 25 years
d. never

10 In 1922, five men stole a delivery truck parked outside the Denver Mint that contained about **$200,000** in ___ bills.

a. $1
b. $5
c. $100
d. $10,000

11 A rare U.S. penny from 1943 recently sold for ____.

a. $100,000
b. $550,000
c. $1.7 million
d. $3.4 million

12 The Egyptian pyramids contained mummies and priceless treasures. How many stone blocks make up the **Great Pyramid at Giza?**

a. 350,000
b. 775,000
c. 1.6 million
d. 2.3 million

13 True or false? An ounce (28 g) of silver can be made into a piece of wire that stretches 30 miles (48.3 km).

CHECK YOUR ANSWERS ON PAGES 166–167.

And a One, and a Two, and a...

1 What do many conductors use to help the musicians keep time?
- **a.** sword
- **b.** baton
- **c.** whistle
- **d.** laser pointer

2 How many black and white keys are on a piano?
- **a.** 48
- **b.** 68
- **c.** 88
- **d.** 98

3 The word *orchestra* originally comes from a Greek word meaning _____.
- **a.** to dance
- **b.** to laugh
- **c.** to run
- **d.** to paint

4 Similar orchestra instruments are placed in groups called families. How many families are in an orchestra?
- **a.** 1
- **b.** 4
- **c.** 8
- **d.** 12

5 In 2009, a British singing group entered the *Guinness Book of World Records* as the largest musical act to release an album. How many singers were in the group?
- **a.** 159
- **b.** 367
- **c.** 1,694
- **d.** 4,386

6 The kazoo was first introduced to the world at the Georgia State Fair in the U.S.A. in what year?
- **a.** 1821
- **b.** 1852
- **c.** 1920
- **d.** 1958

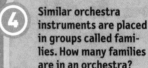

7 Considered a musical genius, Mozart was how old when he first played for the Austrian royal court in Vienna?
a. 3
b. 5
c. 10
d. 15

8 **True or false?** At 158 verses, Greece's national anthem is the longest in the world.

9 Scientists have measured the loudness of a bass drum. It is about as loud as a ___.
a. power mower
b. garbage disposal
c. vacuum cleaner
d. jet taking off

10 **True or false?** The guitar is a modern instrument. It has been around for only 200 years.

11 **True or false?** When a tuba is uncoiled, it is about 6 feet (1.8 m) long.

12 A grand piano can weigh ___ pounds.
a. 100 pounds (45 kg)
b. 500 pounds (227 kg)
c. 1,000 pounds (454 kg)
d. 2,500 pounds (1,134 kg)

13 What was the price tag on the oldest and most expensive violin in the world in 2010?
a. $1 million
b. $6 million
c. $10 million
d. $18 million

14 When a record goes "gold," how many copies of it have been sold?
a. 250,000
b. 500,000
c. 1 million
d. 2 million

CHECK YOUR ANSWERS ON PAGES 166–167.

Know Your Numbers!

1 A HEN, OR FEMALE CHICKEN, CAN PRODUCE ONE EGG IN ABOUT 24 HOURS.

2 GIANT GEORGE IS A STANDARD POODLE WHO STANDS 43 INCHES (109 CM) TALL.

3 THE FASTEST SPEED RECORDED FOR A ONE-MILE (1.6 KM) PIGGYBACK RACE IS 12 MINUTES, 47 SECONDS.

4 A SPECIAL PIZZA OFFERED TO DINERS AT A LONDON RESTAURANT SELLS FOR ABOUT $178.

5 A CANADIAN BOY SET A RECORD BY BALANCING 12 SPOONS ON HIS FACE.

6 A FRISBEE-LOVING DOG NAMED ROSE CAN CATCH UP TO SEVEN FLYING DISCS AND HOLD THEM IN HER MOUTH ALL AT ONCE.

7 A STREET IN REUTLINGEN, GERMANY, IS ABOUT 1 FOOT (30 CM) WIDE AT ITS NARROWEST POINT.

8 THE LARGEST RUBBER DUCK COLLECTION IN THE WORLD BELONGS TO A WOMAN WHO HAS 2,000 OF THE POPULAR BATHTUB TOYS.

9 THE LOUDEST BURP EVER RECORDED WAS ABOUT AS LOUD AS A POWER SAW.

10 A DOG ONCE POPPED 100 BALLOONS WITH HIS MOUTH IN JUST UNDER 45 SECONDS.

11 A GOLF BALL HAS ABOUT 150 DIMPLES ON IT.

12 A TAD, DASH, PINCH, AND SMIDGEN ARE REAL MEASUREMENTS FOR COOKING INGREDIENTS.

13 SHARKS HAVE BEEN AROUND FOR MORE THAN 450 MILLION YEARS.

14 AN ANT CAN LIFT MORE THAN 100 TIMES ITS OWN BODY WEIGHT.

15 THERE IS A SINKHOLE IN CHINA WITH A DEPTH EQUAL TO MORE THAN SEVEN FOOTBALL FIELDS!

16 THE GEYSER KNOWN AS OLD FAITHFUL IN YELLOWSTONE NATIONAL PARK ERUPTS ABOUT ONCE EVERY 90 MINUTES.

17 WHEN A VOLCANO ERUPTS, THE AREA OF GREATEST RISK FOR DEATH AND INJURY IS 20 MILES (32 KM) IN ALL DIRECTIONS.

18 THERE IS A BOOK IN THE U.S. LIBRARY OF CONGRESS THAT IS ABOUT THE SIZE OF THE PERIOD AT THE END OF THIS SENTENCE.

19 A SNOW LEOPARD CAN JUMP ABOUT 50 FEET (15 M).

20 THE SURFACE OF THE SUN IS 1,000° FAHRENHEIT (538°C).

21 SIX STANDARD LEGO BRICKS CAN BE ASSEMBLED ABOUT 100 DIFFERENT WAYS.

22 THE LIFESPAN OF A DOLPHIN IS ABOUT 50 YEARS.

23 SINCE 1957, ABOUT 250 SATELLITES HAVE BEEN LAUNCHED INTO SPACE.

24 THE WORLD'S TALLEST SKYSCRAPER, THE BURJ KHALIFA, IS 2,716 FEET (828 M) HIGH.

25 THERE ARE 555 STEPS TO THE TOP OF THE WASHINGTON MONUMENT IN WASHINGTON, D.C., U.S.A.

26 A MONARCH BUTTERFLY BORN IN THE SUMMER LIVES AROUND 6 TO 8 MONTHS.

27 AMERICANS EAT ABOUT 12 POUNDS (5 KG) OF CHOCOLATE PER PERSON EVERY YEAR.

28 THE RECORD NUMBER OF POINTS SCORED IN AN NBA GAME IS 100.

29 A GOOGOL IS A REALLY BIG NUMBER.

30 A HOWLER MONKEY CAN BE HEARD UP TO 3 MILES (5 KM) AWAY.

CHECK YOUR ANSWERS ON PAGES 166–167.

TRIVIA TECH ZONE

1 For its 1982 "Person of the Year," U.S. magazine Time put _____ on its cover.

a. a bald eagle
b. the space shuttle
c. a computer
d. a race car

2 Which country leads the world in Internet usage with more than **500 million** users?

a. Japan
b. South Africa
c. United States
d. China

3 Apple announced that as of February 2013, more than _____ songs had been downloaded from its music store, iTunes.

a. 1 million
b. 55 million
c. 25 billion
d. 1 trillion

4 About how many **computers existed** in the world in 1953?

a. 0
b. 1
c. 100
d. 1 million

6 "Tweets," brief messages sent via Twitter, must be how many characters or fewer?

a. 140
b. 188
c. 210
d. 570

5 In 2012, Facebook reached _____ billion users!

a. 1
b. 10
c. 100
d. 890

7 True or false? As of 2012, YouTube received about 4 billion views per day.

8 Melissa Thompson of England set a world record for text-messaging speed by typing a **26-word** sentence in _____.

a. 1.3 seconds
b. 25.94 seconds
c. 1 minute, 5 seconds
d. 3.7 minutes

9
AlphaDog is a **robot designed** to go into battle with military troops. It can trek over rough terrain for 20 miles (32.2 km) while carrying _____ of gear.

a. 40 pounds (18 kg)
b. 140 pounds (64 kg)
c. 250 pounds (113 kg)
d. 400 pounds (181 kg)

10
True or false? In 2006, an Australian citizen tried to sell the nation of New Zealand through eBay, with a starting bid of 1 cent.

11
In 1981, twelve engineers at IBM secretly developed the first personal computer (PC). What was their code name?

a. Dirty Dozen
b. 12 Brains
c. Magnificent Minds
d. Dozen Darlings

12
Four game players in Austria hold the world's record for longest video game marathon using a **mobile phone.** How long did the game last?

a. 3 hours, 15 minutes
b. 6 hours
c. 12 hours, 8 minutes
d. 24 hours, 10 minutes

A CIRCUIT BOARD DIRECTING ELECTRICAL CURRENT WITHIN A COMPUTER

CHECK YOUR ANSWERS ON PAGES 166–167.

MAP MANIA!

NATIONS BY THE NUMBERS

1 NORWAY

Norway has the world's most expensive postage stamp. How much does it cost to mail a letter in that country?

a. $.56 (3.26 KR)
b. $1.25 (7.28 KR)
c. $1.67 (9.72 KR)
d. $3.45 (20 KR)

BORHAUG, NORWAY

2 CHINA

In 1974, farmers uncovered life-size clay soldiers and horses that had been buried for more than 2,000 years. Since then, how many figures have been unearthed?

a. 750
b. 1,000
c. 8,000
d. 150,000

RED SQUARE, MOSCOW, RUSSIA

3 RUSSIA

The largest country in the world, Russia, has coasts on which three oceans?

a. Atlantic, Pacific, Indian
b. Pacific, Indian, Arctic
c. Atlantic, Pacific, Arctic
d. Indian, Arctic, Atlantic

TERRACOTTA WARRIORS, XI'AN, CHINA

NORTH AMERICA

ATLANTIC OCEAN

PACIFIC OCEAN

SOUTH AMERICA

D

Do you know these nations by their numbers? Test your knowledge now!

④ CHILE

True or false? An earthquake that struck Chile in 1960 was the most powerful one ever recorded.

PARINACOTA VOLCANO, CHILE

⑤ AUSTRALIA

One of the largest landmasses on Earth, Australia has about the same population as _____.

a. Japan
b. Turkey
c. England, U.K.
d. New York State, U.S.A.

OPERA HOUSE, SYDNEY, AUSTRALIA

ARCTIC OCEAN

E

C

EUROPE

F

ASIA

A

A

AFRICA

PACIFIC OCEAN

INDIAN OCEAN

B AUSTRALIA

ANTARCTICA

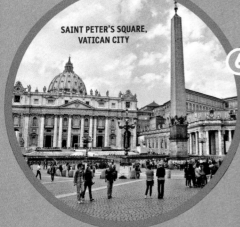

SAINT PETER'S SQUARE, VATICAN CITY

⑥ VATICAN CITY

True or false? Vatican City, an independent nation that is the seat of the Roman Catholic Church, is the smallest nation in the world.

7–12

MATCH THE COUNTRIES IN THE QUESTIONS TO THEIR LOCATIONS ON THE MAP.

CHECK YOUR ANSWERS ON PAGES 166–167.

GAME SHOW

ULTIMATE NUMBER CHALLENGE

1 **TRUE OR FALSE?**
A woodpecker pecks about 8,000 to 12,000 times per day.

2 With more than a dozen factories, Pakistan is the world's leading manufacturer of which musical instrument?
a. kettle drum
b. bagpipes
c. steel guitar
d. clarinet

3 How many eggs were in the world's largest omelet?
a. 36
b. 984
c. 79,100
d. 145,000

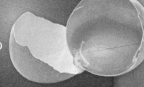

4 How much popcorn does the average American eat in one year?
a. 6 quarts (5.6 L)
b. 54 quarts (51 L)
c. 100 quarts (95 L)
d. 986 quarts (933 L)

5 **TRUE OR FALSE?**
More than 1,500 people participated in the world's largest tug-of-war tournament.

6 The Grand Canyon is believed to be about how old?
a. 17 million years
b. 6 million years
c. 20 million years
d. 35 million years

7 In what year did William Walter build the first robot?
a. 1948
b. 1963
c. 1981
d. 2001

8 A grasshopper can hop how many times the length of its body?
a. 20
b. 50
c. 80
d. 100

9 **TRUE OR FALSE?**
Many skyscrapers do not number their 13th floor.

10 The saying "Leaves of three? Let them be!" is meant to warn people away from _____.
a. oak trees
b. poison ivy
c. stinging nettles
d. bees

11 **TRUE OR FALSE?**
Lake Superior contains about 10 percent of Earth's fresh water.

12 Which of these species has existed since before the time of the dinosaurs?

a.
Bottlenose dolphin

b.
German shepherd

c.
Leafcutter ant

d.
Horseshoe crab

13 **TRUE OR FALSE?**
A Canadian stuntwoman set a record for riding a motorized toilet at 46 miles per hour (75 km/h).

14 Jonathan the tortoise is believed to be the world's oldest living animal at _____ years old.
a. 77
b. 102
c. 256
d. 181

15 **ULTIMATE BRAIN BUSTER**
WHICH CREATURE CAN EAT UP TO 1,200 MOSQUITOES IN AN HOUR?

a.
brown bat

b.
wasp

c.
armadillo

d.
monarch butterfly

Body Parts

1 If you could line up all the blood vessels in the human body, they would be long enough to wrap around the world _____ times.

a. 2½
b. 4
c. 3½
d. 1

2 Some people with vision loss can improve their sight by using a tiny video camera mounted on their _____ that sends signals to their brain.

a. wristbands
b. necklaces
c. headbands
d. sunglasses

3 On average, a person's heart pumps enough blood every day to fill_____.

a. a milk carton
b. a swimming pool
c. a tanker truck
d. three supertanker ships

5 What is the strongest muscle in the human body?

a. leg muscle
b. little toe
c. tongue
d. arm muscle

4 What does the medical term *rhinotillexomania* refer to? [Hint: The prefix *rhino-* refers to the nose]

a. fascination with plastic surgery on the nose
b. obsessive nose picking
c. fear of rhinoceroses
d. an excessively large nose

6 True or false? It's impossible to tickle yourself.

7 About how many bacteria are on each inch of the average person's skin?

a. 32 million
b. 1 million
c. 100,000
d. 700

8 According to a common myth, what is it impossible to do with your eyes open?

a. walk backward
b. kiss
c. sneeze
d. touch your nose

9 Which ordinary item are scientists now using to create artificial bone?

a. inkjet printer
b. food processor
c. electric toothbrush
d. microwave oven

10 What two body parts never stop growing, even into old age?

a. nose and ears
b. eyes and teeth
c. feet and hands
d. brain and heart

11 For how long would you have to constantly pass gas in order to create the energy of an atomic bomb?

a. 6¾ years
b. 19½ years
c. 25 years
d. 9¾ years

12 A kid's heart is about the size of his or her _____.

a. foot
b. fist
c. brain
d. stomach

13 About how many pounds of bugs does the average human accidentally eat each year?

a. 40
b. 30
c. 10
d. 5

Creepy Creatures of the Deep

1 Bombs away! Bomber worms have a unique defense system. What do they release when they are in danger?
a. black ink
b. sharp spikes
c. slimy mucus balls
d. green glowing body parts

2 On land, the mythical Yeti is also known as the Abominable Snowman. What type of animal that lives in the sea (at right) is also called Yeti?
a. Yeti crab
b. Yeti sea monkey
c. Yeti sea snail
d. Yeti tube worm

HAGFISH

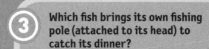

3 Which fish brings its own fishing pole (attached to its head) to catch its dinner?
a. anglerfish
b. pole fish
c. unicorn fish
d. salmon

4 Stay away from the hagfish! When threatened by a predator, it ties itself into a knot and turns the water around it into _____.
a. slime
b. ink
c. poison
d. acid

5 Which type of shark uses its oversized teeth to gouge its prey's flesh like an ice cream scoop?
a. vegetarian shark
b. hammerhead shark
c. cookie cutter shark
d. nurse shark

6 Dragonfish are cool to look at, but what special ability do these deep-sea hunters have?
a. They breathe fire.
b. They emit a red laser-like light.
c. They shoot dart-like spikes.
d. They spear prey with their long tongue.

DRAGONFISH

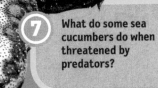

SEA CUCUMBER

7 What do some sea cucumbers do when threatened by predators?

a. They change colors.
b. They release spear-like claws.
c. They poop out their internal organs.
d. They grow larger.

FATHEAD SCULPIN

8 One type of sea worm, sometimes called the "bone-eating snot flower," also has this nickname because it eats skeletal remains.

a. gulper worm
b. zombie worm
c. sucker worm
d. blood worm

9 What is the nickname for this fish, otherwise known as a fathead sculpin?

a. Icky Fishy
b. Mr. Blobby
c. Butterball
d. Cow of the Sea

SEA ANGEL

10 Deep beneath the sea lives the tiny sea angel. What kind of ocean animal is it?

a. a fish
b. a jelly
c. a sea star
d. a snail

11 The rarely seen flabby whalefish lives more than a mile (1.6 km) below the ocean's surface around which country in the South Pacific?

a. Nigeria
b. Fiji
c. New Zealand
d. India

12 **True or false?** Ninety percent of sea creatures living deep in the sea (below 650 feet [200 m]) can make their own light.

FLABBY WHALEFISH

CHECK YOUR ANSWERS ON PAGES 167–168.

127

TEXT ME...LOL ☺

1 **What percent of people admit to texting from the bathroom?**

a. 75 percent   c. 37 percent
b. 53 percent   d. 21 percent

2 **About how many text messages are sent each month in the United States?**

a. 18 trillion   c. 1 million
b. 184 billion   d. 1,500

3 **The average teenage boy sends about 50 text messages a day. How many text messages does the average teenage girl send?**

a. 25   c. 100
b. 50   d. 150

4 **True or false? It would take a million human brains to store all of the information on the Internet.**

5 **How many cell phones each year are thrown away or recycled in the United States because they become damaged or outdated?**

a. 1 million   c. 100 million
b. 50 million   d. 1 billion

6 **In 1992, an engineer from England named Neil Papworth sent the very first text message in the world. What cheerful message did he send?**

a. I love you
b. Please reply
c. First text message
d. Merry Christmas

7 In 1993, an engineer sent the first text message in the United States. What was the embarrassing message?

a. Go USA!
b. Burp
c. Hello...ttyl
d. Text me back

8 About how many page views does Facebook get per minute worldwide?

a. 500
b. 500,000
c. 1 million
d. 6 million

9 What is the busiest day of the year for texting?

a. St. Patrick's Day
b. Valentine's Day
c. New Year's Day
d. Independence Day

10 In which country do people send the most text messages?

a. United States
b. China
c. Philippines
d. Switzerland

11 How long do most people use their new cell phones before losing or replacing them?

a. 9 months
b. 18 months
c. 21 months
d. 2 years

12 True or false? The text acronym LOL ("laugh out loud") is now an entry in the *Oxford English Dictionary*.

13 Ninety-five percent of all text messages travel from the sender to the recipient in ____ seconds.

a. 10
b. 30
c. 60
d. 160

CHECK YOUR ANSWERS ON PAGES 167–168.

Bugging Out

1. Houseflies can taste with their _____.
   a. feet
   b. ears
   c. tongue
   c. wings

TERMITE QUEEN

2. **True or false?** Honeybees kill more people each year than snakes.

3. How many eggs can a termite queen lay every day?
   a. 10
   b. 300
   c. 5,000
   d. 30,000

4. Where might you find the ears of certain types of crickets and grasshoppers?
   a. under the tail
   b. on the head
   c. on the front legs
   d. at the ends of the antennae

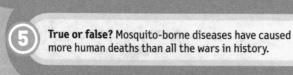

GOLIATH BEETLE

5. **True or false?** Mosquito-borne diseases have caused more human deaths than all the wars in history.

6. What is the smallest insect on Earth?
   a. a stink bug
   b. a fairyfly
   c. a no-see-um
   d. a fire ant

7. Goliath beetles found in Africa are Earth's heaviest insects. How much do they weigh?
   a. 2 ounces (57 grams)
   b. 4 ounces (113 grams)
   c. 8 ounces (226 grams)
   d. 1 pound (.5 kg)

8 What is the name of Earth's biggest spider, which is 11 inches (28 cm) wide with one-inch (2.5 cm) fangs and eight eyes?

a. dino spider
b. Goliath birdeater tarantula
c. Guatemalan huntsman spider
d. camel spider

9 How many insect species do scientists know of so far?

a. 300,000
b. 500,000
c. 1 million
d. 1.5 million

10 What is the only insect on Earth with only one ear?

a. elephant beetle
b. praying mantis
c. stick bug
d. ant

FLIK, FROM A BUG'S LIFE

11 **True or false?** One little brown bat can eat 10,000 to 20,000 insects in one night.

12 Pound for pound (kg for kg), which is the world's strongest animal?

a. dragonfly
b. Goliath birdeater tarantula
c. flea
d. rhinoceros beetle

13 A famous fossil found in Bolivia in 1979 preserves a dragonfly that lived 250 million years ago and was the biggest insect ever known. How wide was its wingspan?

a. as wide as your hand
b. as wide as your foot is long
c. as wide as a ruler is long
d. as wide as a skateboard is long

FOSSILIZED DRAGONFLY

CHECK YOUR ANSWERS ON PAGES 167–168.

TRUE or FALSE?

Out of This World

1 THE SUN HAS BEEN SHINING FOR ABOUT FIVE BILLION YEARS.

2 TODAY'S CELL PHONES HAVE MORE COMPUTING POWER THAN THE COMPUTERS USED DURING THE APOLLO SPACE MISSIONS (1967–1972).

3 THE MOON IS ROUGHLY THE SAME SIZE AS EARTH.

4 THERE ARE ABOUT 50 BILLION STARS IN THE MILKY WAY GALAXY.

5 IN SPACE, BURPS COME OUT WET. YUCK!

6 IF YOU WERE TO TRAVEL TO THE MOON SOMEDAY, YOUR WEIGHT WOULD BE ONE-SIXTH OF WHAT IT IS ON EARTH.

7 MILLIONS OF PIECES OF SPACE JUNK WHIZ AROUND EARTH AT A SPEED OF 15,000 MILES AN HOUR (24,140 KM/H).

8 THE LARGEST DIAMOND IN OUR GALAXY IS A STAR THAT HAS BEEN NICKNAMED "LUCY."

9 EARTH'S MOON IS SLOWLY DRIFTING AWAY FROM OUR PLANET.

10 IF A MILITARY BATTLE TOOK PLACE IN SPACE, IT WOULD BE VERY LOUD.

11 IN SPACE, LIQUIDS FORM TINY SPHERES, OR BALLS.

12 PLUTO WAS DEMOTED FROM A PLANET TO A DWARF PLANET BECAUSE IT WAS THE ONLY PLANET WITHOUT A MOON.

13 EARTH WEIGHS ABOUT 13,170,000,000,000,000,000,000,000 POUNDS (5,974,000,000,000,000,000,000,000 KG).

14 A DAY ON MERCURY IS EQUAL TO ABOUT TWO EARTH MONTHS.

15 A DAY ON THE MOON IS MORE THAN 600 HOURS LONG.

16 GALILEO INVENTED THE TELESCOPE.

17 IT SNOWS ON MARS.

18 VENUS IS THE ONLY PLANET IN OUR SOLAR SYSTEM THAT SPINS BACKWARD.

19 THE FIRST LIVING CREATURE FROM EARTH TO TRAVEL INTO SPACE WAS A DOG NAMED LAIKA.

20 HEADS UP! ONE PIECE OF SPACE DEBRIS FALLS BACK TO EARTH EVERY DAY.

21 SATURN IS THE ONLY PLANET IN OUR SOLAR SYSTEM WITH RINGS.

22 THE SUN IS A THOUSAND TIMES LARGER THAN EARTH.

23 MONS OLYMPUS ON THE PLANET JUPITER IS THE BIGGEST VOLCANO IN OUR SOLAR SYSTEM.

24 SCIENTISTS ARE CURRENTLY WORKING ON A GRAVITY TRACTOR THAT WILL BE USED TO KEEP NEAR-EARTH OBJECTS FROM CRASHING TO OUR SURFACE.

25 THE SUN WILL CONTINUE TO SHINE FOR ANOTHER FIVE BILLION YEARS.

26 STARS HAVE A LIFE CYCLE OF BIRTH, GROWTH, AND DEATH.

27 STARS DON'T REALLY TWINKLE.

28 GIUSEPPE PIAZZI DISCOVERED THE FIRST ASTEROID IN 1801.

29 A BLACK HOLE SUCKS UP EVERYTHING AROUND IT, LIKE A GIANT VACUUM CLEANER.

30 YOU COULD FIT 1.3 MILLION EARTH-SIZE PLANETS INSIDE THE SUN.

CHECK YOUR ANSWERS ON PAGES 167–168.

TEST YOUR ECO-SMARTS

1 About how much water does the average person use in one day?

a. 10–20 gallons (38–76 L)

b. 30–40 gallons (114–151 L)

c. 60–80 gallons (227–303 L)

d. 80–100 gallons (303–379 L)

2 How many airplanes could be built from the aluminum cans thrown out by U.S. airlines in just one year?

a. 1

b. 8

c. 23

d. 58

3 About how many gallons of water did the average person use in one day in medieval times?

a. 5

b. 10

c. 15

d. 30

4 Which product do Americans use at a rate of 1,500 a second?

a. paper

b. plastic forks

c. plastic water bottles

d. sheets of toilet paper

5 What should you not put into a compost bin?

a. egg shells

b. motor oil

c. coffee grounds

d. newspaper

6 About 80 million Hershey's Kisses are wrapped in aluminum foil each day. How many acres could this cover?

a. 50 (20 ha)

b. 25 (10 ha)

c. 5 (2 ha)

d. 100 (40 ha)

7 How many pounds of paper does the average American use in one year?

a. 170 pounds (77 kg) (about one tree)
b. 500 pounds (227 kg) (about three trees)
c. 700 pounds (318 kg) (about four trees)
d. 850 pounds (386 kg) (about five trees)

8 Americans throw out about 300 million tires every year. How many tires are tossed worldwide?

a. 600 million
b. 900 million
c. 1 billion
d. 10 billion

9 True or false? Seventy percent of Earth's surface is covered with water.

10 How much carbon dioxide does one tree absorb from the atmosphere in its lifetime?

a. 1 ton (907 kg)
b. 500 pounds (227 kg)
c. 100 pounds (45 kg)
d. 20 pounds (9 kg)

11 When a glass object is thrown out instead of recycled, how long does it take to decompose?

a. 6 months
b. 10 years
c. 4,000 years
d. over 1 million years

12 What is the most frequently recycled item?

a. plastic water bottles
b. aluminum beverage cans
c. newspapers
d. car batteries

13 What is it called when you give items to others who need them instead of throwing them away?

a. recycling
b. regifting
c. freecycling
d. uploading

14 How many pounds of garbage does the average human toss each year?

a. 2,000 pounds (907 kg)
b. 1,500 pounds (680 kg)
c. 300 pounds (136 kg)
d. 200 pounds (91 kg)

15 True or false? Before the 20th century, bones were the most recycled items.

CHECK YOUR ANSWERS ON PAGES 167–168.

Amazing PLANTS

VENUS
FLY TRAP

1 Where is the only place you will find meat-eating Venus fly traps growing in the wild?
a. along the Yangtze River in China
b. in peat bogs in northern England
c. Central Park in New York City, U.S.A.
d. on the coast of North and South Carolina, U.S.A.

2 What is the most poisonous plant in North America?
a. water hemlock
b. alum lily
c. boysenberry
d. white oak

3 What fruit works better at waking you up than coffee?
a. prunes
b. blueberries
c. apples
d. bananas

4 The corpse flower attracts pollinators with the fragrance of _____.
a. fresh brewed coffee
b. rose petals
c. decaying flesh
d. rotten eggs

CORPSE FLOWER

5 What is the cow's udder plant, a native to South America, sometimes used for?
a. detergent for clothes
b. drinking gourds
c. baby bottles
d. heart medicine

COW'S UDDER
PLANT

6 What plant product can be deadly when eaten by dogs?
a. jelly
b. chocolate
c. apple juice
d. peanut butter

7 **True or false?** The giant water lily is so strong it can support the weight of a human being.

GIANT WATER LILY

8 What type of fruit is most like a pawpaw?
a. orange
b. mango
c. banana
d. peach

9 Have a fire hose ready if you eat this pepper. What is the world's hottest chili pepper?
a. ghost pepper
b. Moruga scorpion pepper
c. pimento pepper
d. green bell pepper

10 The *Wolffia angusta*, a type of duckweed, is one of the world's tiniest plants. A dozen of the plants will fit on a _____.
a. quarter
b. hockey puck
c. pinhead
d. toenail

11 What important product is the foxglove plant used for?
a. herbal tea
b. cough medicine
c. heart medicine
d. skin cream

FOXGLOVE PLANT

12 **True or false?** Almost all high-quality violins are made from African blackwood trees.

CHECK YOUR ANSWERS ON PAGES 167–168.

MAP MANIA!
Fantastic Fossil Finds

Test your knowledge of ancient fossils discovered around the globe.

1 ITALY

What is the name of the mummified human body (shown at right) discovered in 1991 by two hikers?

a. Ötzi the Iceman
b. Olaf the Great
c. Ricky the Ranger
d. Manny the Herder

2 ETHIOPIA

What name did scientists give to the 3.2-million-year-old human fossil they found in 1974?

a. Pam
b. Lucy
c. Ruby Tuesday
d. Strawberry Fields

3 MADAGASCAR

When scientists found the fossil of a fierce 10-pound (4.5-kg) frog that hopped on Earth 70 million years ago, what did they name it?

a. Froggy the Gremlin
b. Kermit
c. devil dog
d. devil frog

4 ENGLAND

True or false? When the first dinosaur bone was found in a quarry in 1676, it was mistakenly thought to be the bone of an elephant.

NORTH AMERICA

D

ATLANTIC OCEAN

SOUTH AMERICA

PACIFIC OCEAN

Weird SCIENCE

ARCTIC OCEAN

C

B
EUROPE
F
ASIA

A

AFRICA
A

PACIFIC OCEAN

E
INDIAN OCEAN

AUSTRALIA

ANTARCTICA

⑤ SOUTH DAKOTA, U.S.A.

The most complete *T. rex* fossil ever found was uncovered in 1990. Now displayed in Chicago's Field Museum (above), the fossil is affectionately called _____.

a. Wilma
b. Sue
c. Jane
d. Fred

⑥ RUSSIA

In what frozen part of the world have scientists recently found a perfectly preserved baby mammoth?

a. Greenland
b. Newfoundland
c. Nebraska
d. Siberia

7–12 MATCH EACH OF THESE LOCATIONS TO THE CORRECT ORANGE AREA ON THE MAP.

CHECK YOUR ANSWERS ON PAGES 167–168.

GAME SHOW

ULTIMATE SCIENCE CHALLENGE

1 At which North American fossil site did lots of prehistoric animals get into a sticky situation and become trapped?
a. Coastal Redwood Forest
b. La Brea Tar Pits
c. Howe Dinosaur Quarry
d. Ogalalla Formation

2 In text language, what does "BRB—P911" mean?
a. Bring the right book. There's a fire.
b. Be right back. Parents are coming in room.
c. Bye for now. Playing game.
d. Be ready by nine o'clock.

3 TRUE OR FALSE?
The world's largest coral reef, the Great Barrier Reef, is visible from space.

4 TRUE OR FALSE?
Fleas can jump 200 times their body length.

5 The rosy periwinkle grows in the Madagascar rain forest. What is it used for?
a. treating childhood leukemia
b. treating migraine headaches
c. making perfumes
d. all of the above

6 The world's largest living organism is a sequoia tree found in Sequoia National Park, California, U.S.A. What is its nickname?
a. Big Red
b. Palm Tree Pete
c. Jerry
d. General Sherman

7 TRUE OR FALSE?
One ton of recycled paper saves 17 trees.

8 How much fuel was left when Apollo 11 landed on the moon?
a. one hour's worth
b. one day's worth
c. 30 minutes worth
d. 20 seconds worth

9 Can you name this bug?
a. orchid mantis
b. lobster cricket
c. chimney cricket
d. iris grasshopper

10 In the average person's lifetime, he or she makes enough saliva to fill two _____.
a. coffee cups
b. bathtubs
c. gallon milk containers
d. swimming pools

11 If Facebook were a country, where would it rank among world populations?
a. most populous
b. second most populous
c. third most populous
d. fourth most populous

12 Halley's Comet last came into view in 1986. When will you be able to see it again as it returns within Earth's view?
a. 2021
b. 2045
c. 2061
d. 2096

13 What substance that hardens over time has kept insects preserved for thousands of years?
a. maple syrup
b. rubber
c. tree sap
d. rock

14 What is one way to reduce the size of your carbon footprint?
a. riding your bike to school
b. picking up trash
c. brushing your teeth twice a day
d. eating an apple every day

15 What was the nickname of the first submersible built to withstand the crushing weight of the ocean's depths?
a. Theodore
b. Simon
c. Alvin
d. Dave

16 ULTIMATE BRAIN BUSTER

WHICH ANIMAL FLIPPED FOR JOY WHEN IT RECEIVED THE RUBBER TAIL THAT SAVED ITS LIFE?

a.
Shamu, the whale

b.
Fuji, the dolphin

c.
Heidi, the opossum

d.
Xiang Xiang, the panda

CHECK YOUR ANSWERS ON PAGES 167–168.

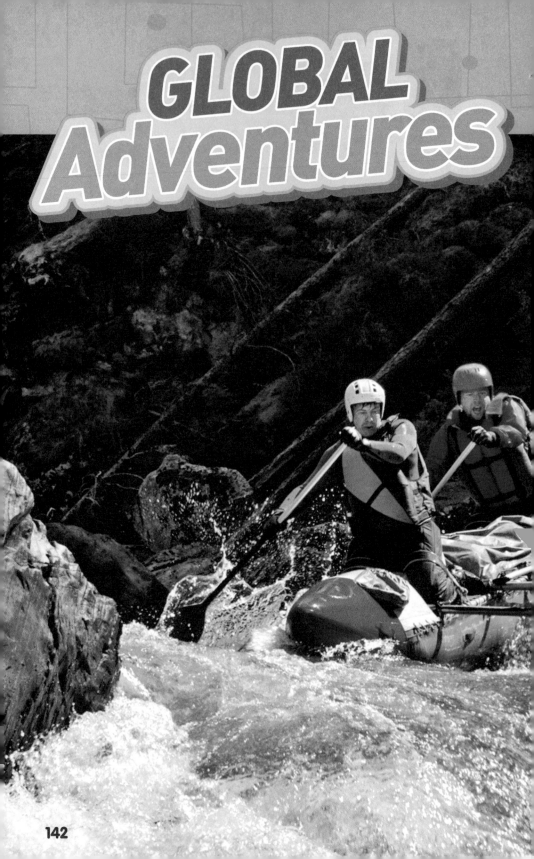

GLOBAL Adventures

Only in America

1. **True or false?** At Crater of Diamonds State Park in Murfreesboro, Arkansas, you can dig for diamonds and keep whatever you find— no matter how big.

2. In what state can you find both the easternmost and westernmost points in the United States?
   a. Nebraska
   b. Alaska
   c. Maine
   d. California

3. The oldest living tree in North America is thousands of years old and has a secret location in the mountains of which American state?
   a. California
   b. Utah
   c. Arkansas
   d. Texas

4. Where is the only place on Earth where alligators and crocodiles live side by side in nature?
   a. Bayou, Louisiana
   b. Everglades, Florida
   c. Cedar Swamp, Oregon
   d. Carlisle Bog, Alaska

ALLIGATOR

5. What sport that people play in Maryland lets you "horse around"?
   a. fishing
   b. basketball
   c. jousting
   d. football

6. An artist makes a cow sculpture out of butter each year at the Iowa State Fair. How much butter does it take to make a life-size butter cow?
   a. 10 pounds (5 kg)
   b. 50 pounds (23 kg)
   c. 100 pounds (45 kg)
   d. 600 pounds (272 kg)

7 True or false? Smokey the Bear was named after a real bear cub that was rescued from a New Mexico, U.S.A., forest fire.

8 The world's largest potato chip is found in this city, which is called the "Potato Capital of the World."

a. Carson City, Nevada
b. Ames, Iowa
c. Portland, Maine
d. Blackfoot, Idaho

9 What state has both the highest point (Mount Whitney) and lowest point (Death Valley) in the continental United States?

a. California
b. Colorado
c. Illinois
d. Kansas

10 In what state can you find the world's largest underground cave—the 400-mile (644-km) long Mammoth Cave system?

a. Indiana
b. Kentucky
c. Nevada
d. Arizona

11 Atlantic City, New Jersey, was the inspiration for a board game. What game was it?

a. Monopoly
b. Scrabble
c. Chutes and Ladders
d. Stratego

12 You can visit the home of PEZ candy in Orange, Connecticut. Which character(s) were featured on top of 2012 PEZ dispensers?

a. Animal, Miss Piggy, and Kermit
b. Homer Simpson
c. Garfield
d. Batman and Robin

13 Ice cream cones, hot dogs, and iced tea became popular at what city's world fair in 1904, before the city's famous arch was built?

a. Paris, Texas
b. Anchorage, Alaska
c. Macdonaldville, Idaho
d. St. Louis, Missouri

14 True or false? There are no states named after U.S. presidents.

15 True or false? The only palace on American soil is 'Iolani Palace (at right) in Honolulu, Hawaii.

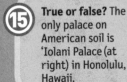

CHECK YOUR ANSWERS ON PAGE 169

Olympics AROUND THE WORLD

1 The Olympic motto is three words that encourage an athlete to do his or her best. What are they?

a. faster, higher, stronger
b. gold, silver, bronze
c. race, sweat, hydrate
d. work, compete, win

2 How many different national anthems were recorded for the 2012 Summer Olympics in London?

a. 0
b. 39
c. 205
d. 5,006

3 Which athlete has won the most Olympic medals ever?

a. Larisa Latynina
b. Michael Phelps
c. David Beckham
d. Venus Williams

4 What did third-place winners receive in the first modern Olympics in 1896 in Athens, Greece?

a. a bronze-colored ribbon
b. nothing
c. $100
d. a gyro sandwich

5 The youngest Olympian ever was gymnast Dimitrios Loundras of Greece, who competed in 1896. How old was he?

a. 2
b. 10
c. 14
d. 16

6 In 1960 at the Summer Olympics in Rome, Italy, Abebe Bikila was the first African to win a gold medal in the marathon. What made Abebe's run extra special?

a. He ran it barefoot.
b. He ran it backward.
c. He was dressed in a fur coat.
d. He had never run before.

8 The very first Olympic Games can be traced back to _____.

a. 1301
b. 776 B.C.
c. 1972
d. 1896

10 In the ancient Olympics the victors did not receive medals. What was their reward for winning?

a. a trophy
b. an olive branch wreath
c. dinner with the emperor
d. an all-expenses-paid trip to the Caribbean

7 Which of these activities was once an Olympic sport?

a. treasure hunting
b. tug-of-war
c. potato sack race
d. tightrope walking

9 True or false? In 1900, first-place Olympic winners in Paris won paintings instead of medals.

11 Gymnast Nadia Comaneci competed at the Montreal Summer Olympics in 1976. What is she best known for?

a. first to receive a perfect 10 score
b. first to perform in a sparkly leotard
c. first to fall off the balance beam
d. first to cry during an Olympic ceremony

12 What percent of an Olympic gold medal is actually gold?

a. 100 percent
b. 90 percent
c. 50 percent
d. 1 percent

CHECK YOUR ANSWERS ON PAGE 169.

Rolling on the River

1 YOU MUST TRAVEL TO AFRICA TO FIND THE DEEPEST RIVER IN THE WORLD, THE CONGO RIVER.

2 MOST RIVERS FLOW FROM NORTH TO SOUTH, BUT THE NILE RIVER FLOWS FROM SOUTH TO NORTH.

3 AUTHOR MARK TWAIN WORKED ON A STEAMBOAT ON THE MISSISSIPPI RIVER, WHERE SOME OF HIS STORY ABOUT HUCK FINN TAKES PLACE.

4 LAKE CHARGOGGAGOGGMANCHAOGGAGOGGCHAUBUNAGUHGAMAUGG IN WEBSTER, MASSACHUSETTS, HAS THE LONGEST PLACE NAME IN THE UNITED STATES, BUT NOT THE WORLD.

5 THE MEKONG RIVER RUNS THROUGH SIX COUNTRIES—CHINA, BURMA, VIETNAM, LAOS, CAMBODIA, AND THAILAND.

6 IN 1901, ANNIE EDSON TAYLOR, AT 63 YEARS OLD, WAS THE FIRST PERSON TO GO OVER NIAGARA FALLS IN A BARREL AND SURVIVE.

7 FEW PEOPLE KNOW ABOUT THE "SECRET RIVER" (CALLED RIO SECRETO) IN MEXICO BECAUSE IT IS HIDDEN IN A JUNGLE.

8 THE DEAD SEA, LOCATED BETWEEN ISRAEL AND JORDAN, IS ACTUALLY A LAKE.

9 IF YOU WANT AN EASY RIVER FLOAT FROM ONE PLACE TO ANOTHER ON A RAFT, YOU CHOOSE A TRIP THAT TAKES YOU "UPRIVER."

10 ON FLORIDA RIVERS, BOATS AND BARGES ARE MORE DANGEROUS TO MANATEES THAN ALLIGATORS ARE.

11 EXPLORER HENRY HUDSON "ACCIDENTALLY" FOUND THE HUDSON RIVER WHILE LOOKING FOR A ROUTE TO CHINA.

12 AFRICAN AMERICANS TRAVELED THE RIVER JORDAN TO ESCAPE BANDITS IN THE UNITED STATES DURING THE 1800s.

13 THE GANGES RIVER IS CONSIDERED THE HOLY RIVER OF INDIA.

14 THE BOTTOM OF A RIVER IS CALLED THE *SOLE*, LIKE THE SOLE OF A SHOE.

15 PEOPLE IN RUSSIA TIPTOE ALONG RIVERS SO THAT THEY DO NOT DISTURB FISH LAYING EGGS.

16 AMAZON RIVER DOLPHINS IN SOUTH AMERICA COME IN ALL SHADES OF PINK.

17 THE GRAND CANYON IN ARIZONA WAS FORMED BY A LARGE LAKE THAT DRIED UP OVER TIME.

18 THERE ARE NO BRIDGES ACROSS THE MAIN STEM OF THE AMAZON RIVER IN NORTHERN SOUTH AMERICA.

19 THE SIDES OF A RIVER ARE CALLED THE *BANKS*.

20 PEOPLE HAVE USED HYDROPOWER, THE ENERGY CREATED FROM FALLING WATER, FOR MORE THAN 2,000 YEARS.

21 GIANT SNAKES CALLED ANACONDAS WAIT FOR THEIR PREY IN SOUTH AMERICAN RIVERS.

22 THE GREAT SALT LAKE IN UTAH ACTUALLY HAS FRESH WATER.

23 GRAVITY MAKES A RIVER FLOW BY PULLING THE WATER DOWNHILL.

24 LOUISIANA HAS THE LARGEST SWAMP IN THE UNITED STATES.

25 THE MISSISSIPPI RIVER IS THE LONGEST RIVER IN THE UNITED STATES.

26 A WATERFALL CAN NEVER FREEZE.

27 THERE IS ENOUGH CONCRETE IN THE HOOVER DAM IN THE WESTERN UNITED STATES TO PAVE A HIGHWAY FROM SAN FRANCISCO TO NEW YORK.

28 IT TAKES MORE THAN 300 YEARS FOR A DROPLET OF WATER TO MAKE ITS WAY THROUGH ALL FIVE OF THE GREAT LAKES.

29 THE NILE RIVER IS CALLED "THE CRADLE OF CIVILIZATION."

30 THE YELLOW RIVER IN CHINA IS CONSIDERED TO BE THE WORLD'S CLEAREST RIVER.

CHECK YOUR ANSWERS ON PAGE 169.

Cool Facts About CHINA

1 What percent of the entire world population lives in China?

a. 25%   c. 20%
b. 33%   d. 50%

2 True or false? Ping-Pong was not invented in China.

4 Some people say this treat was invented in China about 4,000 years ago, when a mixture of milk and rice was frozen in snow.

a. fortune cookies   c. snow cones
b. ice cream   d. cottage cheese

3 True or false? There are 26 letters in the Chinese written language.

5 What essential item was invented by the Chinese for their emperor in the late 1300s?

a. lead pencil   c. toilet paper
b. cell phone   d. hairbrush

6 Which animal is considered a national treasure in China

a. giant panda   c. giraffe
b. snow monkey   d. bald eagle

7 What did the Chinese make in the 1100s by stuffing gunpowder into bamboo tubes and then setting them on fire?

a. cannons
b. fireworks
c. flashbulbs
d. candles

8 What famous Italian explorer traveled to China in the 1200s and brought ivory, jade, and silk back to Europe?

a. Han Solo
b. Marco Polo
c. Gulliver
d. Hannibal

9 True or false? Thousands of workers who died while building the Great Wall of China are buried within the wall.

10 In 1974, an army of thousands of clay soldiers was found buried in China. What did they guard?

a. a large treasure chest
b. the grave of the First Emperor
c. the royal silkworms
d. an awesome restaurant

11 What fictional creatures are held in high regard in China?

a. dragons
b. fairies
c. trolls
d. unicorns

12 What color symbolizes good luck and happiness in China?

a. gray
b. green
c. black
d. red

Traveling CIRCUS

1 About how fast does a human cannonball fly through the air?
a. 20 miles per hour (32 km/h)
b. 30 miles per hour (48 km/h)
c. 70 miles per hour (113 km/h)
d. 100 miles per hour (161 km/h)

2 What food do circus performers consider bad luck and never eat before a performance?
a. peanuts
b. popcorn
c. hot dogs
d. pretzels

3 What might circus performers keep in their pockets because it is good luck?
a. rabbit's foot
b. elephant hair
c. tiger tail
d. horse's mane

4 What is the average size of a clown's shoe?
a. 10
b. 14
c. 18EE
d. 26EEEE

5 Vivian Wheeler is famous for what facial feature?
a. big red nose
b. one large hairy eyebrow
c. most number of freckles
d. 11-inch (28-cm) beard

6 This nickname will make your skin crawl! Even though they love them, what do circus performers call their fans?
a. circus spiders
b. lot lice
c. fan fleas
d. clapping ants

7 Everybody loves the circus! What U.S. president traveled to Philadelphia to see the first American circus?

a. Alexander Hamilton
b. John F. Kennedy
c. Franklin D. Roosevelt
d. George Washington

8 **True or false?** For good luck, circus performers always jump into the ring with both feet.

9 A Frenchman, Jules Leotard, strung cords and a bar over a swimming pool in 1859 and invented what circus act?

a. juggling
b. clowning
c. flying trapeze
d. tightrope walk

CIRCUS
PERFORMERS

10 **True or false?** Bozo the Clown, a popular TV show character during the 1960s, was not one clown, but many different actors playing the character.

11 What will get a circus performer sent out of a dressing room and forced to turn around three times before being allowed back in?

a. whistling
b. crying
c. singing
d. talking

12 What is considered to bring bad luck during a circus parade?

a. waving to the crowd
b. looking backward
c. shaking hands
d. signing autographs

13 Which U.S. president declared National Clown Week to be the first week of August?

a. Richard Nixon
b. Barack Obama
c. Herbert Hoover
d. Thomas Jefferson

14 Sore throats were probably common among performers in which country, where sword swallowing began thousands of years ago?

a. Mexico
b. Canada
c. Norway
d. India

CHECK YOUR ANSWERS ON PAGE 169.

MAP MANIA!
SCUBA SIGHTS

PTOLEMAIC KING STATUE, PORT OF ALEXANDRIA

① PORT ROYAL, JAMAICA

Called the "Wickedest City on Earth," most of this city slid into the sea on June 7, 1692, when an earthquake shook the area. What group of people lived here?

a. Jamaican royalty
b. pirates
c. prisoners
d. fishermen

② MICRONESIA

Ships sank in the Pacific Ocean during World War II. Today some of them in the Chuuk Lagoon in Micronesia attract divers because of their beauty. What makes them so colorful?

a. bright paint
b. pink sand
c. rainbows
d. coral

③ PORT OF ALEXANDRIA, EGYPT

What ancient site is preserved in the shallow waters of the Port of Alexandria, Egypt?

a. City of Troy
b. El Dorado, the lost city of gold
c. Dracula's castle
d. Cleopatra's palace

④ WINDOVER POND, FLORIDA, U.S.A.

Less than 50 miles from Florida's Disney World is Windover Pond. What can you find there?

a. Goofy's buried bones
b. alligator farms
c. Donald Duck's birthplace
d. Native American burial site

NORTH AMERICA

ATLANTIC OCEAN

SOUTH AMERICA

PACIFIC OCEAN

G

B

F

GLOBAL Adventures

There are many wonderful things to see on Earth's surface. But did you know there are some amazing lost cities and sunken ships on the ocean floor? Throw on your scuba gear and take this quick tour of just a few of the wonders preserved underwater.

⑤ ATLANTIC OCEAN

What famous ship hit an iceberg and now rests several hundred miles off the coast of Nova Scotia.

a. Titanic
b. Republic
c. Lusitania
d. Queen Elizabeth II

⑥ BAIAE, ITALY

Most of the ruins of the ancient Roman city of Baiae are underwater. Like Pompeii, a natural force submerged this portion of the city. What was it?

a. a meteor
b. a flood
c. an earthquake
d. volcanic activity

⑦ CHINA

What ancient city, guarded by large lion statues, lies 90 feet (27 m) below the surface of Qiandao Lake in southeastern China?

a. Lion City
b. Simba City
c. Ho Chi Minh City
d. Atlantis

8–14 MATCH THE LOCATION OF EACH OF THE UNDERWATER WONDERS TO THE CORRECT RED MARKER ON THE MAP.

ARCTIC OCEAN

EUROPE
ASIA
C
E
D
AFRICA
PACIFIC OCEAN
A
INDIAN OCEAN
AUSTRALIA
ANTARCTICA

GAME SHOW
ULTIMATE GLOBAL CHALLENGE

1 In a recent survey, who (or what) was voted the most famous figure in Scotland?

a. Prince Harry
b. Loch Ness monster

c. Bigfoot
d. Mary, Queen of Scots

2 How many Empire State Buildings could you stack in Lake Baikal, the world's deepest lake?
a. 1
b. 8
c. 3
d. 10

3 What country has the most medals from the Winter Olympic Games?
a. U.S.A.
b. Mexico
c. Italy
d. Norway

4 TRUE OR FALSE?
When the S.S. *Central America*, nicknamed the "Ship of Gold," sank off the coast of North Carolina, it took 21 tons (19 tonnes) of gold down with it.

5 The Iditarod is a 1,150-mile (1,850 km) race by dog sled. Where could you see this race?
a. Dikson, Russia
b. Narsaq, Greenland
c. Alaska, U.S.A.
d. Reykjavik, Iceland

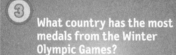

6 If you wanted to hunt for treasure near where the famous pirate Blackbeard once lived, where should you go?
a. Missouri
b. Colorado
c. North Carolina
d. Texas

CAPTAIN EDWARD TEACH, KNOWN AS BLACKBEARD

7 What name is used for the huge tents used by traveling circuses?
a. The Big Umbrella
b. The Big Top
c. The Fun Tent
d. The Big House

8 Milk is the official drink of which American state?
a. Wisconsin
b. North Dakota
c. Virginia
d. Texas

9 Vending machines in Nanjing, China, sell about _____ live crabs a day.
a. 200
b. 100
c. 5
d. 0

10 What mythical sunken city beneath the sea has never been found, but researchers keep on looking for its location?
a. Agrabah
b. Atlantis
c. Floating Gardens
d. Gondor

11 TRUE OR FALSE?
Years ago, artists competed in the Olympic Games.

12 What word describes something very large and comes from the name of a famous elephant in P.T. Barnum's traveling circus?
a. Jumbo
b. Humongous
c. Mambo
d. Biggie

13 What famous landmark shoots anywhere from 3,700 to 8,400 gallons (14,006 to 31,797 L) of boiling hot water into the air every hour or two?
a. Old Faithful, Wyoming
b. Mt. St. Helens, Washington
c. World's Largest Teapot, West Virginia
d. Teapot Dome, Michigan

15 ULTIMATE BRAIN BUSTER

WHAT DID A TIGHTROPE WALKER CROSS OVER IN 2012?
a. the Nile River
b. Niagara Falls
c. the Mariana Trench
d. Antarctica

14 TRUE OR FALSE?
In ancient China, anyone caught taking silkworm eggs out of the country was put to death.

TIGHTROPE WALKER PRACTICING OVER CITY STREET

CHECK YOUR ANSWERS ON PAGE 169.

ANSWERS

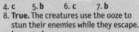

Animal KINGDOM

The Wild Life, pages 10–11

1. c
2. **True.** Blue whales grow up to 100 feet (30 meters) long and can weigh 200 tons (181.4 tonnes).
3. d   4. c
5. **True.** Elephant calves are born blind, with only their trunks to navigate and explore.
6. a   7. b   8. a   9. d
10. **False.** The echidna is another mammal that reproduces by laying eggs.
11. b   12. c

Catching Some ZZZs, pages 12–13

1. c   2. b
3. **True.** Tigers can't always eat a large animal in one meal, so they sleep next to their food until they have eaten all the meat.
4. d   5. d   6. a   7. a
8. **True.** This technique allows the animals to stay alert for predators.
9. c   10. c   11. a
12. b   13. a
14. **False.** An open mouth allows for temperature regulation.
15. d

Hi, Honey, I'm Home!, pages 14–15

1. d   2. c
3. **True.** In ancient Greece and Rome, people believed that the honey cakes were needed to get past Cerberus, the three-headed dog guarding the underworld.
4. **False.** The queen bee stays in the hive while the worker bees go out and collect pollen from flowers.
5. d   6. a   7. b   8. c
9. c   10. b   11. c   12. a
13. **True.** The entire hive must work together to make larger amounts of honey. A hive produces 30 pounds or more of honey per year.
14. d   15. c

And Now for My Next Trick... pages 16–17

1. a   2. b
3. **True.** The stones help grind the meat they have eaten.

4. c   5. b   6. c   7. b
8. **True.** The creatures use the ooze to stun their enemies while they escape.
9. b   10. d   11. c
12. **False.** Spiders spin webs in different shapes, and some do not spin webs at all.
13. a

What's for Dinner?, pages 18–19

1. a   2. c
3. d
4. **False.** They can only drink blood. It makes up their entire diet.
5. b   6. d
7. a   8. d
9. **True.** Energy in a food chain starts with the sun, moves to plants, and then through the animals that eat it.
10. c   11. b   12. c   13. d

Map Mania! Pals in Peril, pages 20–21

1. J—eastern Australia
2. I—parts of Indonesia and southeast Asia
3. C—Amazon basin, South America
4. F—parts of western and central Africa
5. D—Brazil, South America
6. B—California, Arizona, and Utah, U.S.A.
7. A—Arctic coastlines; some islands in Greenland and Canada
8. G—central and southern Africa
9. H—Madagascar
10. E—Asia (also parts of Europe and North America, not marked on map)

Egg-cellent Animals, pages 22–23

1. a   2. a   3. a   4. c
5. c   6. c   7. b   8. a
9. b   10. c   11. b   12. b
13. **False.** Chicks hatch throughout the year.
14. d

Going Ape, pages 24–25

1. **True.** A gorilla's nose leaves a unique print.
2. d   3. b
4. **False.** Gorillas are mainly herbivores, eating fruit, leaves, seeds, and stems of plants.
5. b
6. **True.** Scientists have seen gorillas use tools, including sticks, to test the depth of streams.
7. a   8. c
9. **True.** Gorillas and adult humans have 32 teeth.
10. a   11. a   12. b   13. c

What's a Body to Do?, pages 26–27

1. c   2. d
3. **True.** The four sharpest teeth in humans and other mammals are called canines, and they are meant for biting into and holding on to foods. "Canine" is another word for "dog."
4. d   5. c   6. b   7. c
8. **False.** Quills are defenses against enemies, but porcupines cannot aim or shoot the quills out of their bodies. They are released when a porcupine is touched. Don't touch!
9. a   10. d   11. a
12. **True.** A fly's eye is called a compound eye, which contains many tiny eyes and lenses within it that help the insect detect movement and avoid predators.

True or False? Home Sweet Home, pages 28–29

1. **True.** The bromeliad, a rain forest plant, collects pools of water in its leaves, providing a home for some animals, including the tree frog.
2. **True.** The deep sea gets no sunlight, but some animals use bioluminescence, which is a chemical reaction that lets an animal's body give off light.
3. **False.** Ants don't live in Antarctica.
4. **False.** Polar bears live in the Arctic region, and penguins live in the Antarctic region.
5. **True.** "Super colonies" of ants can live in a region thousands of miles wide.
6. **True.** The mangrove killifish can survive out of the water for about 66 days because it can breathe oxygen through air, as well as through water.
7. **False.** Skunks are nocturnal animals. This means they are only active and away from their homes at night.
8. **False.** Animals that live underground live in burrows or dens.
9. **True.** The Baltimore oriole, for example, migrates 3,000 miles (4,828 km) from its summer home in the United States to its winter home in South America.
10. **True.** The females, called nannies, may live with as many as 20 children, called kids, at one time.
11. **True.** The arctic fox has a white coat in winter to match the snow. It has a brown coat in summer to match the brown dirt.
12. **False.** Animals that live in caves permanently, such as the cavefish, are partially or totally blind.
13. **True.** The pupfish survives the winters by burrowing into the muddy bottoms of bodies of waters.
14. **False.** Wolves are social animals that live and travel in groups called packs.
15. **True.** The London Underground mosquito is believed to have adapted itself to the cool, urban environment in which it lives.
16. **True.** This owl lives inside the trunks of

the giant saguaro cacti in the Sonoran Desert in the southwestern United States.

17. **True.** The naked mole rat spends most of its time digging tunnels—miles long—in the deserts of East Africa.

18. **True.** There are some 35,000 stray dogs living in Moscow's subway system!

19. **True.** Birds called oxpeckers eat insects off the hippo's skin. Herons and egrets sit on the hippo's back to catch fish.

20. **False.** Toucans live in rain forest environments.

21. **False.** Gray foxes make dens in hollow tree logs as well as caves.

22. **True.** The Arizona bark scorpion lives in cities or urban environments.

23. **True.** Wild boars have been able to find food in the city and live in the many parks and gardens.

24. **True.** The bark beetle lives in tree bark, often causing harm to the tree.

25. **True.** After the eggs hatch, worker ants

move the larvae to a new chamber and feed them until they become pupae.

26. **False.** Real roadrunners live in the southwestern United States.

27. **True.** Coral reefs support a lot of life but cover less than one percent of the ocean floor.

28. **False.** The climate of Antarctica is too cold for snakes to survive.

29. **True.** Weasels called ferrets often prey on prairie dogs and then move into their underground burrows.

30. **False.** Alligators live in warmer climates than porcupines.

Game Show: Ultimate Animal Challenge, pages 30–31

1. a   2. a   3. d
4. c   5. c
6. **True.** A male platypus has a retractable

"stinger" that it uses to defend itself against enemies and against rivals for a female.

7. a   8. b   9. a
10. **False.** The flying squirrel looks like it is flying, but it does not have wings. It can glide 150 feet (45 meters) through the air by stretching its skin like a parachute using its arms and legs.

11. d   12. d
13. c   14. a
15. **Pangolin**

SCORING

What on EARTH?

Coast to Coast, pages 34–35

1. c
2. **True.** The first horses arrived in Australia in 1788 by boat with the first Irish and British settlers.
3. b   4. c   5. a
6. **False.** Sand dunes are made up of loose sand formed into mounds by the wind, and are found in deserts, on beaches, and even on Mars!
7. **True.** The appearance of a sea cliff depends on the kind of rock that makes up the wall. Some cliffs have rounded domes while others form more jagged edges.
8. b   9. b   10. b
11. **False.** Scientists estimate that there are about ten times more stars in the sky than grains of sand on Earth, including all the sand in deserts and on beaches!

12. c   13. c
14. **True.** The length of Canada's coastline is over 124,000 miles (200,000 km). How long is Poland's coastline? It's 273.4 miles (440 km).
15. d

Mark Your Calendar, pages 36–37

1. c   2. a
3. d   4. a
5. **True.** Many cultures hold this celebration to welcome spring.
6. b   7. b
8. **False.** A day on Mars is about 40 minutes longer than a day on Earth.
9. c

10. **True.** In France, the one who is being pranked is called *poisson d'avril* for "April fish." The term may have originated from a reference to a young fish that is easily caught.
11. b   12. a   13. c

Be a Good Sport!, pages 38–39

1. **True.** The event takes place in Gloucestershire, and even though it was officially canceled in 2010, an unofficial Cheese Rolling has continued.
2. a
3. **True.** Invented in 1993, Blo-ball is like table tennis without the paddles or the net. The game requires players to try to blow the ball past their opponent.
4. b   5. c   6. b
7. **True.** Between the years 1900 and 1920, tug-of-war was an Olympic event.
8. c   9. b   10. d
11. a   12. d

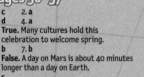

True or False? On Location, pages 40–41

1. **True.** Katharine Lee Bates, inspired by Colorado's Rocky Mountains, penned the famous lyrics in 1893 when visiting Pikes Peak.
2. **False.** The Amazon River is located in South America and is 3,977 miles (6,400 km) long.
3. **False.** Admiral Richard Byrd made five successful Antarctic expeditions beginning in 1928.
4. **True.** This first-ever wax infant at Madame Tussauds is on display at the museum's New York City location.
5. **True.** Stolen from the Louvre museum in Paris in 1911, the *Mona Lisa* was returned in 1913 when the thief was caught trying to sell it.
6. **True.** Mount Fuji last erupted in 1707 but is still considered an active volcano.
7. **True.** Located in India, the Taj Mahal took more than 20 years to build and is adorned with many different varieties of precious stones. Elephants were used to transport construction materials.
8. **False.** The 21st Winter Olympic Games were held in Vancouver in 2010.
9. **False.** Located just south of the Great Pyramid of Giza in Egypt, the Great Sphinx has the face of a man and the body of a lion.
10. **False.** The British Open, which began in 1860, is actually the world's oldest golf championship.
11. **False.** Wooden shoes, or clogs, worn by the Dutch are a popular souvenir for visitors to the Netherlands. The word *Dutch* refers to the people from the Netherlands.
12. **True.** The Forbidden City, where common people were once forbidden to enter, is a maze of structures in Beijing, China. It dates back to the 1400s and has been home to many emperors.
13. **True.** Built for the 1889 World's Fair, the airy structure is now a beloved symbol of Paris.
14. **True.** Galešnjak, a small island in the Adriatic Sea off the coast of Croatia, was first noticed for its heart shape after its image was captured on Google Earth.
15. **True.** The Cancun Underwater Museum features man-made underwater sculptures and is a popular tourist attraction for divers and art lovers.
16. **False.** There are five Great Lakes: Lake Superior, Lake Michigan, Lake Huron, Lake Ontario, and Lake Erie.
17. **True.** Tinker Bell's flight begins over Cinderella's Castle in the Magic Kingdom.
18. **True.** The city of Venice, Italy, is actually 118 small islands connected by canals.
19. **True.** This unusual hotel, located in the country of Sri Lanka, sleeps up to ten people in the belly of an elephant made from grass and twigs.
20. **True.** Watching the snakes being milked of their venom is one of the many popular activities at the Rattlesnake Roundup.
21. **False.** The ancient Colosseum in Rome has not hosted a major event in more than a thousand years.
22. **True.** More than a thousand gallons (4,000 L) of blue paint were used to cover the buildings in Júzcar, Spain, for the movie premiere in 2011.
23. **False.** Washington's nose is 20 feet (6 m) long, several feet less than an average school bus, which is about 38 feet (11.5 m).
24. **False.** "Aloha!" is a greeting you might hear in Hawaii. It can mean *hello* as well as *good-bye*!
25. **False.** A popular legend about St. Patrick is that he rid Ireland of snakes by driving them into the sea.
26. **True.** Some say that Insano is a perfect name for this 135-foot (41-m) tall water slide because you would have to be insane to ride it!
27. **True.** Scientists are trying to learn whether the cave paintings were made by Neanderthals, who appeared on Earth about 200,000 years ago in Europe.
28. **False.** In the Harry Potter books, Hogwarts is located in Scotland.
29. **True.** The sun is still shining at midnight in June in Iceland.
30. **True.** Stretching across northern Africa, the Sahara is the world's largest nonpolar desert and is roughly the same size as the continental United States.

Let's Talk Tradition!, pages 42–43

1. b
2. **True.** The top of the head is considered the place where one's spirit lives, and it's a personal insult to touch anyone there.
3. c   4. d
5. **True.** In Japan, speaking to someone while keeping your hands in your pockets is considered very rude.
6. c
7. **True.** Competitors must wear a horse collar around their necks while making the most grotesque face they can. The tradition dates back to 1267.
8. a
9. **False.** Recent evidence suggests that fortune cookies originated in Japan. Made of sesame and miso, *tsujiura senbei* (fortune crackers) held the paper fortunes in the outer folds of the treats.
10. d
11. **True.** Old dishes are thrown at the homes of friends. Many broken dishes means a person has many good friends.
12. b

Take Me to Your Leader, pages 44–45

1. a   2. c
3. **False.** The famous Fabergé eggs were not chocolate but gold and were decorated with diamonds, rubies, and other jewels.
4. b   5. b
6. **True.** Teddy Roosevelt was 42 when he took office in 1901, after William McKinley's assassination. John F. Kennedy was the youngest ever elected to the office of president, at 43.
7. d   8. c   9. b

10. **True.** Puyi became China's last emperor in 1908 when he was 2 years, 10 months old.
11. **False.** The title shogun was given to military rulers in Japan.

A Capital Idea!, pages 46–47

1. c   2. d   3. a
4. **True.** Pretoria, Cape Town, and Bloemfontein are each home to a different branch of government.
5. b   6. c
7. **True.** Mexico City is a continuation of the Aztec capital of Tenochtitlán, founded in about 1325.
8. c
9. d   10. b
11. **False.** Construction of the White House began when Washington was in office. John Adams was the first president to live in the White House.

Map Mania! Great Adventure, pages 48–49

1. a   2. d   3. d   4. c
5. d   6. b   7. b
8. Zambezi River—F
9. Alaska, U.S.A.—C
10. Antarctica—G
11. Guadalupe Island, Mexico—E
12. Mount Everest—B
13. Australia—D
14. Galápagos Islands—A

Game Show: Ultimate Earthly Challenge, pages 50–51

1. a
2. **False.** Glaciers can be found high in the mountain near the equator in the Andes in South America and the Himalaya in Asia.
3. b   4. b   5. d   6. c
7. **True.** The poisonous fish is considered a delicacy in Japan. A trained chef cleans and prepares it, which (hopefully) removes the poison.
8. a   9. c   10. d
11. c   12. b
13. **True.** The African elephant stands approximately 8.2 to 13 feet (2.5 to 4 m) compared to the Asian elephant at 6.6 to 9.8 ft (2 to 3 m).
14. c   15. d

SCORING

0–44

BICYCLES AND BACKPACKS

It's fun to meet new people, see new sights, and learn new things. If you can get there by bicycle, you're as happy as you can be. But you also know that there's more than one way to travel. Keep a book in your backpack, and you're off on your next adventure!

45–88

ALL ABOARD!

If it has wheels or wings and can move forward, you're ready to jump aboard! Adventure awaits around every corner and the world is wide open to you. When you hear the word *explore*, you say, YES, PLEASE!

89–133

TO THE MOON AND BEYOND!

You plan to travel to every corner of Earth. You want to meet people from every nation in the world, try their foods, learn their languages, and then move on to the next one! And when you cross off the last destination on your lengthy list, you'll set your sights for the stars. You may just be the first tourist to visit Mars!

Pop Culture

Kid TV, pages 54–55

1. c   2. c   3. a   4. d
5. a   6. b   7. d   8. c
9. b   10. a   11. d   12. b
13. c

Famous Villains, pages 56–57

1. b   2. a
3. **False.** Sauron is the enemy of Bilbo and his companions. Gandalf is the wizard who guides and mentors Frodo on his journey.
4. d   5. b   6. d   7. b
8. d   9. d   10. a
11. **False.** Gollum was a Hobbit before being corrupted by the One Ring, but he got his name from the horrible sound he makes in his throat when he speaks.
12. a   13. b   14. c

True or False? Movie Mania!, pages 58–59

1. **False.** Percy must make peace between his father, Zeus, and Hades regarding Zeus' missing lighting bolt.
2. **True.** As of 2012, the *Harry Potter* films have made nearly $8 billion.
3. **False.** In *Diary of a Wimpy Kid: Dog Days*, Greg's a bit too young for beards. He does take part in a pretend Civil War battle, but that's a disaster!
4. **True.** In *ParaNorman*, Norman can speak to the dead, including to his grandmother and the town ghosts.
5. **True.** *Brave*'s Princess Merida loves archery and adventure, not princess-y things, such as sitting still, or wearing clothing that restricts her movement, or having her hair combed.
6. **True.** The coordinates for the Allspark in *Transformers* were imprinted on the glasses of Sam's great grandfather Archibald.
7. **False.** After their plane crashes in France, the four large animals in *Madagascar 3: Europe's Most Wanted* hop onto a circus train to escape Animal Control Officer DuBois and to get back to New York.
8. **False.** In *The Sea of Monsters*, Percy Jackson must find the Golden Fleece in order to save Camp Half-Blood.
9. **True.** As in other *Ice Age* movies, Scrat the Squirrel faces a constant battle in *Ice Age: Continental Drift* with his one prized acorn!
10. **True.** Like the book, which Dr. Seuss published in 1971, the message of the movie *The Lorax* is that unless someone cares, nothing will change.
11. **False.** Jack Black plays the part of Gulliver, a New York newspaper mailroom clerk.
12. **True.** The Pirate Captain has never been crowned Pirate of the Year and sets that as his goal in *The Pirates! Band of Misfits*.
13. **True.** Yes, Timothy is more plant than person.
14. **False.** *Toys in the Attic*, originally produced in the Czech language, is about toys that come to life when no one is watching. Watch the movie in Czech on YouTube!
15. **True.** In *Finding Nemo*, Bruce is a great white shark, Anchor is a hammerhead shark, and Chum is a mako shark.
16. **False.** The Avengers include Marvel Comics superheroes Captain America, Thor, Iron Man, and the Hulk.
17. **True.** In *Cars 2*, the Italian formula racecar driver, Francesco Bernoulli, challenges Lightning McQueen to race in Japan's World Grand Prix.
18. **True.** All three *Lord of the Rings* movies were filmed in New Zealand.
19. **True.** Jackie Chan's character in *The Spy Next Door* wins the heart of beautiful neighbor Gillian, but we never learn his real name!
20. **False.** Captain America is a superhero because he becomes part of a secret program that helps him to run, jump, and lift things with superhuman strength. His indestructible shield comes in pretty handy, too!

21. **False.** In *Tron: Legacy*, Sam Flynn transports himself to the Grid, a virtual reality world created by his father Kevin Flynn, who disappeared 20 years earlier.
22. **False.** The story of *Kung Fu Panda* takes place in China in the fictional Valley of Peace.
23. **False.** Carl uses thousands of balloons to lift up his house.
24. **False.** In the final scene of *Iron Man*, Tony Stark tells reporters that he is Iron Man.
25. **False.** Fans of *The Karate Kid* know that Dre Parker learns the value of growing more calm and mature as he masters more martial arts skills in preparation for the big tournament.
26. **False.** After the genie comes out of the lamp in the collapsed cave, he grants Aladdin three wishes with these three exceptions: no killing people, no forcing people to fall in love, and no bringing the dead back to life.
27. **True.** Harry learns in *Harry Potter and the Deathly Hallows, Part 2* that Snape was his mother Lily's friend and that Snape secretly tried to protect Harry out of respect for Lily Potter.
28. **False.** Dr. Bruce Banner turns into a raging green giant whenever he becomes angry.
29. **False.** Nemo is born in the Great Barrier Reef off the coast of Australia.
30. **False.** Hiccup's dragon friend is named "Toothless" because the dragon can hide its teeth.

Star Struck, pages 60–61
1. **a**   2. **d**
3. **False.** Johnny Depp played the Mad Hatter in *Alice in Wonderland* and Willy Wonka in *Charlie and the Chocolate Factory*.
4. **c**   5. **b**

6. **c**   7. **d**
8. **False.** The British Royal Mail printed their pictures on stamps.
9. **b**
10. **c**
11. **True.** Selena was only seven years old when she first appeared on *Barney & Friends* in 1999.

For Gamers Only!, pages 62–63
1. **a**
2. **False.** Water dragons have flippers and can't walk well.
3. **c**
4. **True.** Stories about people getting swine flu were all over the news at the time of the game's creation.
5. **b**   6. **a**   7. **d**
8. **c**   9. **c.**   10. **a**
11. **b**   12. **b**   13. **b**
14. **c**

Game Show: Ultimate Pop Culture Challenge, pages 64–65
1. **d**   2. **c**
3. **c**   4. **a**
5. **False.** Anton Ego is a restaurant critic.
6. **True.** According to the Entertainment Software Association (ESA), almost half of American households have a game console.

7. **d**
8. **a**
9. **True.** According to YouTube, 70 percent of its traffic comes from outside of the United States. It's watched in 53 countries and the videos are shown in 61 languages.
10. **d**
11. **False.** Andy's toys end up at a daycare center after his mother mistakenly puts them outside on the curb for the garbage truck.
12. **b**   13. **c**

SCORING

0–32
DOING YOUR OWN THING
Keeping up with the latest cartoons and TV shows is just not your thing. You're an individual who doesn't like to follow the crowd. But you're also someone who soaks up new information like a Transformer, or you would not be looking at this book!

33–65
THE RIGHT BALANCE
You don't like to miss your favorite TV shows or the newest movie or latest game, but you also spend time with other things. Balancing your interests keeps you smart and happy.

66–95
YOU'RE A SUPERSTAR!
There isn't a movie you haven't seen or a game technology you haven't used. People go to you for facts on pop culture and technology. You are a true Quiz Whiz!

Get Back to NATURE

Survival Guide, pages 68–69

1. a   2. d
3. **True.** A person can survive in the wilderness by eating a variety of insects, fish, birds, and small mammals. Don't try this at home—or anywhere!
4. b
5. **False.** Rubbing frostbitten skin will damage the tissue further. Get your toes into warm—not hot—water.
6. a   7. c
8. **False.** The inner bark of pine trees contains sugars, starches, and calories. People have scraped and cooked it so that it can be digested.
9. a
10. **True.** Small fish such as minnows can be scooped up with a T-shirt. Larger fish can be speared with a stick.
11. a   12. b   13. a   14. a

It's a Cookout!, pages 70–71

1. b   2. d
3. **True.** Ketchup can be used to clean items made of copper. The salt and acid in the tomatoes eats away at stains in copper.
4. c   5. d   6. d
7. **False.** Pies can be made on a grill as well as baked in an oven.
8. b
9. c   10. b   11. c
12. **True.** Hot dogs were a food on Apollo flights to the moon, space shuttle flights, and other space missions.

A Starry Show, pages 72–73

1. a   2. c   3. b   4. b
5. **False.** We see different constellations from Earth during different times of the year due to Earth's position in its orbit around the sun.
6. b
7. **True.** The constellation called Orion, the hunter, gets its name from Greek mythology.
8. d   9. a
10. **False.** Stars can only be seen through a clear sky with little or no clouds.
11. d   12. b   13. d   14. a

Map Mania! Wild Weather, pages 74–75

1. a   2. b   3. b
4. d   5. c   6. d

7. Extreme dry weather—E—Atacama Desert, Chile, South America
8. Sandstorm—D—Sahara desert, North Africa
9. Monsoon—B—Southern Asia
10. Heat wave—F—Northwest and Central Australia
11. Hurricane—C—Atlantic Coast, U.S.
12. Tornado—A—Tornado Alley, United States

Amazing Antarctica, pages 76–77

1. d   2. b
3. **True.** The average wind speeds are 50 miles per hour (80 km/h).
4. b   5. b
6. **False.** Antarctica is a continent with no countries. The land has been managed under an international treaty since 1959. Today, 50 countries are part of the treaty.
7. c   8. b
9. c
10. **False.** In fact, more than 60 species of insects live in Antarctica.
11. d   12. a

True or False? Out at Sea, pages 78–79

1. **True.** The colossal squid can be more than 43 feet (13 m) long.
2. **False.** Less than 10 percent of the world's oceans have been explored.
3. **False.** An octopus has three hearts.
4. **False.** The blue whale's heart is about the size of a small car.
5. **True.** The orca, the largest member of the dolphin family, has a black-and-white coloring that is easy to identify.
6. **True.** The deeper someone goes in the ocean, the greater the force of water pressure will be.
7. **False.** The largest ocean is the Pacific, which covers about 30 percent of the planet's surface.
8. **False.** About 3.5 billion people (about half the world's population) get their primary source of protein from the ocean.
9. **True.** A mako shark can swim 60 mph (97 km/h).
10. **True.** The underground mountain range is more than 40,000 miles (64,400 km) long.
11. **False.** A tablespoon of seawater contains millions of bacteria and many thousands of phytoplankton and zooplankton.
12. **False.** The speed of sound through water is almost five times faster than it is through air.

13. **True.** The world's oceans contain about 20 million tons (18 million tonnes) of gold.
14. **True.** An octopus has blue blood.
15. **False.** Ninety percent of the Earth's volcanic activity happens in the ocean.
16. **True.** Scientists have currently named 219,000 species, according to the World Register of Marine Species.
17. **True.** The ocean's top ten feet (3 m) of water hold as much heat as in the entire atmosphere of Earth.
18. **False.** Earthquakes under the sea can cause tsunamis.
19. **True.** Sea levels have increased on average about 4–10 inches (10–25 cm) over the past 100 years.
20. **True.** The Atlantic Ocean is named after Atlas, a character from Greek mythology.
21. **True.** In 1985, Jacques Mayol, also known as the "Dolphin Man," set the record depth of 344 feet (105 meters).
22. **True.** With more than 25,000 islands, the Pacific Ocean has more than the rest of the world combined.
23. **False.** Most offshore oil drilling occurs in the Arabian Gulf, the North Sea, and the Gulf of Mexico.
24. **True.** Blue whales are larger than any known dinosaurs.
25. **True.** The gray whale migrates 10,000 miles (16,100 km) per year.
26. **True.** The moon's gravitational pull on Earth causes oceans to bulge out toward the moon.
27. **True.** Organisms that live in hydrothermal vents on the ocean floor may be used to make new cancer-fighting drugs.
28. **False.** The letters in the word *SCUBA* stand for "self-contained underwater-breathing apparatus."
29. **False.** The Arctic Ocean is nearly completely covered by ice in the winter, not the summer.
30. **True.** Coral and human bones share chemical and physical structures; as a result, some doctors have used coral instead of bone grafts in operations.

A Distinct Desert, pages 80–81

1. a
2. **True.** The venom of a desert rattlesnake is very potent and requires about 20 vials of antivenom, a medicine made from the venom of the snake.
3. c
4. **True.** They are bitter, and a jackrabbit will only eat the leaves if it has nothing else to eat.
5. a   6. c   7. b
8. b   9. c
10. **False.** Only about 500 kinds of plants in the Sonoran Desert are edible.
11. c
12. **True.** It can get this hot in the area near the tip of Mexico.
13. c   14. b

Game Show: Ultimate Nature Challenge, pages 82–83

1. a 2. c
3. **True.** Four stars make up the bowl of the dipper, and three stars make up the handle.
4. a 5. b
6. **False.** Tropical storms and hurricanes are named in alphabetical order, so the first storm of the season starts with the letter *A*.
7. c 8. d 9. a
10. **True.** Even though the sun is 93 million miles (150 million km) from Earth, it is the star closest to our planet.
11. d 12. b 13. c

SCORING

0–40
OUT TO LUNCH
Your score shows that you may be more comfortable planning a picnic than planning a mission to the Mariana Trench or planet Mars. Look around at nature while you flip those burgers. Soon you'll be able to tell a white oak from a white dwarf.

41–80
YOU'RE LEARNING THE ROPES
You know quite a few things about the driest, coldest, wettest, and stormiest places on the planet … and beyond. Feeling swamped? Get outside a little more and keep learning about the great outdoors.

81–121
YOU'VE REACHED THE TOP
You're outdoorsy for sure. You know much more about nature than any bookworm. You probably know the name of every state bird and the name of every constellation. Use your knowledge to help conserve the natural world or explore outer space.

Blast FROM THE PAST

Flashback!, pages 86–87

1. a
2. **True.** An insurance company hired Harvey Ball to design a happy face to cheer up employees.
3. c 4. b 5. b
6. a 7. b
8. **True.** The Austrian candy maker took the first "p," the middle "e," and final "z" in *pfefferminz* to make the name for the new candy.
9. a 10. b 11. c
12. d 13. d
14. **False.** The LEGO company introduced its classic "brick" toy parts in 1958.

In Knightly Fashion, pages 88–89

1. b 2. b 3. d 4. a
5. **True.** Battle armor had to be strong against weapons but flexible enough for soldiers to move quickly and easily.
6. c
7. **False.** A strong horse could carry a knight in armor, even though the armor alone might weigh 50 pounds (23 kg) or more!
8. **False.** Great heroines, like Joan of Arc, did fight in battles and some wore armor.
9. b 10. c
11. b 12. a
13. d

Rock On!, pages 90–91

1. c 2. a 3. b
4. c 5. d 6. b

7. **False.** Beyoncé is a popular American singer.
8. d 9. b
10. **True.** Music Television soon became known as MTV.
11. a 12. d 13. c 14. b

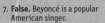

National Parks Road Trip!, pages 92–93

1. d
2. **False.** Canadians make excellent maple syrup, but Banff is known for its beautiful mountains, glaciers, and evergreen forests.
3. **False.** Explorers named the geyser because it faithfully erupts within every two hours. Its water is way too hot for a shower.
4. c 5. a 6. c
7. a 8. a
9. **True.** Dinosaur Provincial Park has fossils from 35 species of dinosaurs!
10. a
11. **True.** People also used the bucket to gather guano to make fertilizer. People rode in it until 1925, when a staircase was built into the cave.

Eat, Drink, and Be Merry!, pages 94–95

1. b   2. d
3. **True.** Herbs we use today, like dill, were used in ancient civilizations to heal the body and try to cure ailments like hiccups.
4. a
5. **True.** A lollipop was a candy that you "popped" onto your "lolly" (British word for *tongue*). The use of sticks for lollipops became widespread in the 1900s.
6. b   7. a   8. d
9. **True.** German peasants had to pay the feudal lords honey and beeswax.
10. d   11. b   12. b   13. b

DragonVille, pages 96–97

1. d   2. a   3. c
4. b   5. b   6. c
7. **True.** Viking sailors were superstitious but not stupid; they took the dragon heads down as they approached land so they wouldn't frighten everybody else!
8. d   9. a   10. c
11. **False.** This line, which Bilbo Baggins says to himself, is quoted from J.R.R. Tolkien's book *The Hobbit*.
12. b
13. **False.** Barney is a large purple dinosaur that stars in the children's television program *Barney & Friends*.

Famous Fiction, pages 98–99

1. a   2. a   3. c   4. b
5. **True.** Before his first children's book was published in 1945, E.B. White fell asleep on a train and dreamed of a boy who looked like a mouse.
6. a   7. b   8. d   9. d
10. **True.** Each of the history stories features a girl from a different era.

11. a
12. **True.** *Esperanza Rising* received many awards for telling the story of Mexican farm workers during the Great Depression of the 1930s.
13. b

Animals Tamed by Time, pages 100–101

1. **True.** The Ancient Egyptians so loved their domesticated cats that they shaved their eyebrows when the family cat died.
2. c
3. **True.** *A domesticated* animal is one that has changed over generations from a wild animal into one that can help work, feed, and clothe people.
4. b   5. d   6. a
7. d   8. a   9. b
10. **False.** Scottish inventor James Watt invented the term *horsepower* to describe how much work his new steam engine could do compared to a horse.
11. c   12. d   13. d   14. a

Map Mania! World Travelers, pages 102–103

1. b   2. d   3. d
4. c   5. c
6. **True.** The ship of Spanish explorer Magellan traveled around South America and then continued west to Spain, proving the world was round.
7. Marco Polo—D—China
8. Hernando de Soto—E—Mississippi River
9. Coronado—F—Arizona and New Mexico
10. Vasco da Gama—B—India
11. Howard Carter—C—Egypt
12. Ferdinand Magellan—A—Strait of Magellan, South America

Game Show: Ultimate Blast from the Past Challenge, pages 104–105

1. d
2. **True.** The Hoover Dam is over 726 feet (221 meters) tall, and the Washington Monument is about 555 feet (169 meters) tall.
3. a   4. a   5. b
6. **False.** Women were not allowed to compete in the Olympics until 1900.
7. d   8. c
9. **True.** In *Mighty Morphin Power Rangers* (1993–1996), the teen superheroes sometimes used a powerful "dragon" shield and other such tools to battle evil forces.
10. d   11. b
12. **True.** Since 1994, Chinook has never been beaten by a human opponent.
13. c   14. b   15. d   16. b

SCORING

0–45

IN THE NOW
Do you live in the moment, too busy to think about the past? Try plugging into both the now and then: Visit a fun museum, or explore the mysteries of your town or your family's past. You can even keep a diary and write your own history!

46–91

IN THE KNOW
You really know your history! And you also know this helps you understand the present. Use valuable information about the past to participate in new things with confidence. History buffs like you have bright futures ahead!

92–133

IN THE "NO WAY!" ZONE
Congratulations, you're an official international treasure! Allow your passion for history to inspire creative ideas. Who knows? You could make history. Think big. The world is waiting for you—lead on!

It All ADDS UP!

Count Your Critters, pages 108–109

1. c 2. b 3. a 4. c
5. **False.** There are 34 living species in the canine family.
6. c 7. a 8. b
9. c 10. d 11. c
12. **True.** Parrots have two toes pointing forward and two toes pointing backward.

Treasure Chest, pages 110–111

1. d 2. b 3. d 4. b
5. a 6. d
7. **True.** The rings and earrings were part of the loot stolen from a jewelry store in 2008.
8. c 9. c 10. b 11. c
12. **c**
13. **True.** An ounce of silver can yield a wire that stretches 30 miles (48.3 km)!

And a One, and a Two, and a..., pages 112–113

1. b 2. c 3. a 4. b
5. d 6. b 7. b
8. **True.** The anthem is based on a lengthy poem with 158 verses.
9. a
10. **False.** The oldest preserved guitar-like instrument belonged to an Egyptian singer over 3,500 years ago and was buried with him.
11. **False.** The tuba is the largest member of the brass family, and if uncoiled it would reach about 18 feet (5.5 m)!
12. c 13. d 14. b

True or False? Know Your Numbers!, pages 114–115

1. **True.** Although some hens rest a few days between laying eggs, some start producing the next egg as soon as 30 minutes later.
2. **False.** Giant George is actually a Great Dane who entered the *Guinness Book of World Records* for World's Tallest Dog in 2010.
3. **True.** The race took place in New York City in 2010.
4. **True.** The pricey pizza is topped with expensive truffles, a rare but very tasty kind of mushroom.
5. **False.** Aaron Caissie actually balanced 17 spoons on his face to set a world record!
6. **True.** The flying discs must be thrown one at a time, but Rosie can hold all seven in her mouth.
7. **True.** The Spreuerhofstrasse was measured in 2006 and was named Narrowest Street by the *Guinness Book of World Records*.
8. **False.** Charlotte Lee has been collecting rubber ducks since 1996. She set a world record by collecting 5,631 of the squeaky toys.
9. **True.** The United Kingdom's Paul Hunn broke the world record in 2009.
10. **True.** A Jack Russell terrier named Anastasia performed the amazing feat on live television in 2008.
11. **False.** Most golf balls have about 392 dimples.
12. **True.** A tad is about 1/8 of a teaspoon, a dash is 1/16, a pinch is 1/24, and a smidgen is about 1/32.
13. **True.** Scientists believe that sharks are older than the dinosaurs!
14. **False.** An ant can lift only about 20 times its body weight, but that is the equivalent of a human lifting a car.
15. **True.** It is believed to be the largest sinkhole in the world!
16. **True.** About 70 years ago, the eruptions at Yellowstone National Park came about every 67 minutes, but over the years the time has increased, probably due to changing underground water levels.
17. **True.** This area is known as the danger zone, but ash clouds from an erupting volcano can spread for hundreds of miles/kilometers.
18. **True.** The book, *Old King Cole*, measures 1/25 inches (1 mm) by 1/25 inches (1 mm).
19. **True.** Snow leopards use their powerful legs for leaping and their long tail for balance.
20. **False.** Actually the sun is even hotter—10,000°F (5,538°C)!
21. **False.** Six 2 x 4 LEGO bricks can be assembled in about 100 million ways!
22. **True.** Porpoises, on the other hand, only live 15 to 20 years.
23. **False.** Over 2,500 satellites have been launched and are used for communications, global positioning, weather predicting, and more!
24. **True.** Not only is the Burj Khalifa the world's tallest building, it is also the world's tallest freestanding building, and it has more than 160 stories.
25. **False.** There are 897 steps to the top, or you can just take the elevator.
26. **False.** The butterfly lives only 6 to 8 weeks.
27. **True.** But the Swiss have Americans beat in chocolate consumption; they eat 22 pounds (10 kg) per person each year.
28. **True.** At 7'1" (1.8 m), Wilt Chamberlain holds the record for most points scored in one game.
29. **True.** A googol is 1 followed by 100 zeroes!
30. **True.** Howlers are some of the larger primates and are known for their loud, distinctive cry.

Trivia Tech Zone, pages 116–117

1. c 2. d 3. c
4. c 5. a 6. a
7. **True.** About 30,000 visitors viewed videos on YouTube each day when it launched in 2005.
8. b 9. d
10. **True.** The bid reached $3,000 before eBay removed it due to policy violation. Apparently countries are not for sale!
11. a 12. d

Map Mania! Nations by the Numbers, pages 118–119

1. c 2. c 3. c
4. **True.** It measured a 9.5 magnitude and caused damage as far away as the west coast of the United States!
5. d
6. **True.** Vatican City in Rome, Italy, is only .2 square miles (.4 km²).

7. Norway – E
8. China – A
9. Russia – C
10. Chile – D
11. Australia – B
12. Vatican City – F

Game Show: Ultimate Number Challenge, pages 120–121

1. **True.** These birds peck on trees to find the insects under the bark.
2. b 3. d 4. b
5. **True.** The competition took place in Rochester, New York, with more than 1,500 people tugging the rope!
6. b 7. a 8. a
9. **True.** Believed to be unlucky by many people, the number 13 is often skipped, so floor numbers go directly from 12 to 14.
10. b
11. **True.** The lake is approximately 10,000 years old and contains more water than all the other Great Lakes combined.
12. d
13. **True.** Stuntwoman Jolene Van Vugt set this record in May 2012.
14. d 15. a

SCORING

0–36

NUMBING NUMBERS

Not everybody is cut out for the numbers game, but that's okay! The world needs word whizzes, too. If you turn *1, 2, 3* into *one, two, three*, you just might figure it all out!

37–73

COOL COUNTER

Your friends can *count* on you to have fun with facts and figures! You like numbers, and you're not afraid to use them. Your mind is like a file cabinet filled with random bits of awesomeness!

74–108

DIGIT DAZZLER

You and numbers are BFFs! That's great! You can rattle off fascinating facts faster than anyone! Examined under a microscope your brain looks like alphabet soup, but with numbers!

Weird SCIENCE

Body Parts, pages 124–125

1. a   2. d   3. b
4. b   5. c
6. **True.** The cerebellum, part of your brain, warns the rest of your brain that you are about to tickle yourself so the sensations are ignored.
7. a   8. c   9. b   10. a
11. a   12. b   13. d

Creepy Creatures of the Deep, pages 126–127

1. d   2. a   3. a   4. a
5. c   6. b   7. c   8. b

---

9. b   10. d   11. c
12. **True.** They are bioluminescent.

Text Me...LOL ☺, pages 128–129

1. a   2. b   3. c
4. **True.** The Internet is estimated to hold about 5 million terabytes of data (5 trillion megabytes) and the human brain is estimated to hold 1 to 10 terabytes of information.
5. c   6. d   7. b
8. d   9. c   10. c
11. b
12. **True.** The acronym first appeared in the *Oxford English Dictionary* in 2011.
13. b

Bugging Out, pages 130–131

1. a
2. **True.** Because many people have serious allergies to bee stings, honeybees kill dozens of people a year in the United States while only a handful of people die from snakebites.
3. d   4. c
5. **True.** The diseases mosquitos carry kill 2–3 million people each year.
6. b   7. b   8. b
9. d   10. b
11. **False.** The brown bat can eat only about 2,000–6,000 insects in a single night.
12. d   13. d

True or False? Out of This World, pages 132–133

1. **True.** The sun has been shining for 4.6 billion years.

---

2. **True.** A single smartphone contains more computing power than all the computers used to send astronauts into space in the 1960s and 1970s.
3. **False.** The moon is actually about one-quarter the size of Earth.
4. **False.** Scientists believe there are about 200 billion stars in the Milky Way galaxy.
5. **True.** Without gravity to separate liquids from gases in the stomach, burps come out wet. For this reason, sodas and other carbonated drinks are not allowed on spacecrafts.
6. **True.** Your weight on the moon would be one-sixth of what it is on Earth due to differences in effects of gravity.
7. **True.** Space junk, such as broken satellites or nuts, bolts, and tools dropped by astronauts, orbiting at high speeds can cause serious damage if it collides with spacecraft or satellites.
8. **True.** The largest diamond in our galaxy is the diamond star, discovered in 2004 and named for a Beatles tune, "Lucy in the Sky with Diamonds."
9. **True.** Scientists have determined that the moon appears to be moving away from Earth about 1.5 inches (3.8 cm) each year.
10. **False.** There is no sound in space due to the lack of air to carry sound waves.
11. **True.** Without gravity, spilled liquids form spheres or blobs. As a result, spills on spacecrafts can't be mopped up but must be chased down and caught with absorbent wipes.
12. **False.** Pluto is now considered a dwarf planet because scientists discovered that it does not have its own orbital path and it shares space with objects close to it in size. Planets do not share space with objects of similar size and they have distinct orbital paths.
13. **True.** Scientists used a mathematical formula to determine this weight.
14. **True.** A day, or the time it takes a planet to rotate on its axis, on Mercury is about 58 Earth days.
15. **True.** A day on the moon is 655.72 hours long.

16. **False.** Galileo used a telescope, but he did not invent it; Hans Lippershey invented the instrument in the early 1600s.
17. **True.** Scientists have found that it snows dry ice on Mars.
18. **True.** Venus spins in the opposite direction of all the other planets in our solar system.
19. **True.** Laika the dog traveled aboard *Sputnik 2* in 1957.
20. **True.** According to officials at NASA, one piece of space debris has fallen to Earth every day for the past 40 years.
21. **False.** Jupiter, Uranus, and Neptune also have rings, but the rings around Saturn are easier to see.
22. **False.** The sun is 100 times the diameter of Earth.
23. **False.** Taller than Mount Everest, Mons Olympus on Mars is the biggest volcano in our solar system.
24. **True.** Rather than use a rocket or bomb to destroy an asteroid or other objects, scientists are developing a way to use gravity to alter the object's course to make it miss Earth.
25. **True.** Our sun is middle-aged and has about another five billion years worth of fuel left to burn.
26. **True.** Although a star is not a living thing, it follows a pattern—from its formation (birth) to its collapse (death)—that is similar to a biological form's life cycle.
27. **True.** Changes in Earth's atmosphere make it look like stars twinkle.
28. **True.** The asteroid was so huge that it was first classified as a planet.
29. **False.** Black holes exert tremendous forces of gravity, which cause all nearby objects to fall into them; the action is more like falling than being sucked or vacuumed up.
30. **True.** The radius of the sun is 109 times larger than the radius of Earth. That means that more than 1 million Earth-size planets could fit inside it.

Test Your Eco-Smarts, pages 134–135
1. **d**   2. **d**   3. **a**   4. **c**
5. **b**   6. **a**   7. **c**   8. **c**
9. **True.** Three-quarters of the Earth is covered with water—but only 1 percent is usable.
10. **a**   11. **d**   12. **b**
13. **c**   14. **b**
15. **True.** Bones were recycled and used for items such as buttons and glue, as well as for food.

Amazing Plants, pages 136–137
1. **d**   2. **a**   3. **c**
4. **c**   5. **a**   6. **b**
7. **True.** The pad of the giant water lily can support up to 300 pounds (136 kg).
8. **c**   9. **b**   10. **c**   11. **c**

12. **True.** Almost all high-quality violins are made from the African blackwood because the wood is hard, shiny, and it creates a bright, loud sound.

Map Mania! Fantastic Fossil Finds, pages 138–139
1. **a**   2. **b**   3. **d**
4. **True.** Robert Plot found the bone and thought it resembled an enormous human bone, so he concluded it must have been the bone of an elephant brought to England by the Romans.
5. **b**   6. **d**
7. Italy—F
8. Ethiopia—A
9. Madagascar—E
10. England—B
11. South Dakota, U.S.A.—D
12. Russia—C

Game Show: Ultimate Science Challenge, pages 140–141
1. **b**   2. **b**
3. **True.** The Great Barrier Reef is the only living thing in the world large enough to be viewed from space.
4. **True.** Because of their specially jointed back legs, fleas can jump to heights that are the equivalent of a human jumping over a 70-story building.
5. **a**   6. **d**
7. **True.** One ton of recycled paper prevents 17 trees from being cut down, as well as the resources used to process each tree into paper.
8. **d**   9. **a**   10. **d**
11. **c**   12. **c**   13. **c**
14. **a**   15. **c**   16. **b**

SCORING

0–45
TRIAL AND ERROR
You're just beginning to experiment and gather information. There's lots of exciting science still to discover. Keep up your curiosity! Visit a local science museum or read a great book to pick up some new facts.

46–91
INVENTING
You know your way around the lab and can't wait for your first big invention. *How* and *why* is what you need to know, and you don't stop until you have all the answers. Just don't create Frankenstein's monster, please.

92–136
BREAKTHROUGH!
Scientists may want to study your brain to see how you learned so much science! (And it's all yours—no brain implants!) Keep up the good work, and you may someday come up with solutions the whole world will remember.

GLOBAL Adventures

Only in America, pages 144–145

1. **True.** The policy here is "finders keepers," but there is a small fee to dig for diamonds.
2. **b**   3. **a**   4. **b**
5. **c**   6. **d**
7. **True.** After being found clinging to a tree following a serious forest fire, the little cub was named "Smokey" and eventually ended up at the National Zoo in Washington, D.C.
8. **d**   9. **a**   10. **b**
11. **a**   12. **a**   13. **d**
14. **False.** There is one state named after a U.S. president—the state of Washington.
15. **True.** It was home to Hawaii's last royalty: King Kalakaua and Queen Liliuokalani.

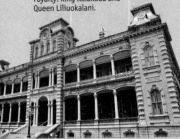

Olympics Around the World, pages 146–147

1. **a**   2. **c**   3. **b**   4. **b**
5. **b**   6. **a**   7. **b**   8. **b**
9. **True.** Paintings were considered more valuable.
10. **b**   11. **a**   12. **b**

True or False? Rolling on the River, pages 148–149

1. **True.** The Congo River has depths of more than 720 feet (219 m).
2. **True.** The Nile River flows from south to north.
3. **True.** Mark Twain worked as a steamboat captain from 1857–1861. (Part of that time he spent as an apprentice.)
4. **True.** The lake is also known as Lake Webster. The city of Bangkok in Thailand has the longest place name in the world if written in the Thai language. The name has 163 letters.
5. **True.** The Mekong River is about 2,700 miles (4,345 km) long.
6. **True.** After surviving the 167-foot (51-m) fall, her comment to others was, "Don't try it."
7. **False.** It gets its name "Secret River" because it flows underground.
8. **True.** The Dead Sea is a saltwater lake.
9. **False.** Going "upriver" means traveling against the flow of the river. If you want an easy float on a raft, go with the flow and float "downriver."
10. **True.** Scientists think alligators may occasionally attack a manatee, but more than half of Florida manatees have been injured by boats or barges.
11. **True.** Hudson traveled about 150 miles (241 km) up the river before realizing he was not on target for China.
12. **False.** "River Jordan" was the code word for the Ohio River, part of the Underground Railroad, which slaves used to escape slavery.
13. **True.** Many people believe that the river can wash away their sins.
14. **False.** It is called the bed.
15. **False.** But at one time, people kept church bells quiet along Russia's Volga River when fish called sturgeon were laying eggs. These eggs are a favorite food and are so valuable they are called "black gold."
16. **True.** They are born gray, but turn pink as they age.
17. **False.** The Colorado River carved the great gorge.
18. **True.** The Amazon mostly runs through the rain forest.
19. **True.** Riverbanks are where the water ends and the land begins.
20. **True.** Today people use water flowing through dams to create electricity. Two thousand years ago, people used it to grind grain.
21. **True.** They can grow to over 28 feet (8.5 m) and up to 500 pounds (227 kg).
22. **False.** It is a saltwater lake, and the water is so salty that fish can't even live in it.
23. **True.** Rivers flow from high places to low places. Gravity causes that flow of water.
24. **True.** The Atchafalaya Swamp in Louisiana is over 1 million acres (400,000 hectares) and has been home to many different cultures, from Native Americans to present-day Cajuns.
25. **False.** The Missouri River is longer than the Mississippi River. The Mississippi is 2,320 miles (3,734 km) long. The Missouri is 2,540 miles (4,088 km) long.
26. **False.** Waterfalls can freeze at a very cold temperature.
27. **True.** There is enough concrete in the Hoover Dam to build a standard highway 16 feet (4.8 m) wide from San Francisco to New York.
28. **True.** From the time it enters Lake Superior to the time it exits into the Atlantic Ocean, a water droplet will have been on a 320-year journey.
29. **True.** The annual flooding of the river left soil on the surrounding land that helped make it fertile, and perfect for the first farmers.
30. **False.** The Yellow River is the muddiest.

Cool Facts About China pages 150–151

1. **c**
2. **True.** Ping-Pong was invented in England, where it is also known as table tennis.
3. **False.** There are over 40,000 characters.
4. **b**   5. **c**   6. **a**   7. **b**
8. **b**
9. **False.** No bodies have ever been found within the wall, but thousands of workers were buried in trenches alongside the wall.
10. **b**   11. **a**   12. **d**

ANSWERS

Traveling Circus, pages 152–153

1. **c**   2. **a**   3. **b**   4. **d**
5. **d**   6. **b**   7. **d**
8. **False.** They always step out on their right foot for good luck.
9. **c**
10. **True.** Bozo the Clown has been played by more than 100 actors over the years.
11. **a**   12. **b**   13. **a**   14. **d**

Map Mania! Scuba Sights, pages 154–155

1. **b**   2. **d**   3. **d**   4. **d**
5. **a**   6. **d**   7. **a**
8. Port Royal, Jamaica—F
9. Micronesia—A
10. Port of Alexandria, Egypt—E
11. Windover Pond, Florida, U.S.A.—B
12. Titanic Wreckage, Atlantic Ocean—G
13. Baiae, Italy—C
14. Qiandao Lake, China—D

Game Show: Ultimate Global Challenge, pages 156–57

1. **b**   2. **c**   3. **d**
4. **True.** When it was discovered in 1988, the gold was worth at least $52 million.
5. **c**   6. **c**   7. **b**
        8. **a**   9. **b**   10. **b**
11. **True.** Between 1912 and 1948, artists won Olympic medals for art that was based on sports.
12. **a**   13. **a**
14. **True.** The Chinese made silk cloth from the strands that wrapped the eggs, and they were very protective of the secret to making silk.
15. **b**

SCORING

76–112

0–37

JUST CHILLING
Your spirit for adventure is still developing. Right now, you don't need to take any big risks because life provides plenty of excitement! As you learn more about what's out in the world, you will go looking for it.

38–75

READY FOR ACTION
You've got a long list of things you want to do, and you're always thinking of how to do them. If it's something new and offbeat, you are into it. Keep up your adventurous spirit and curiosity, and you'll never be bored!

76–112

PUSHING THE LIMITS
You might be skiing the high country, or on a raging river raft trip next weekend. Your can-do spirit and all-purpose knowledge will take you as far as you want to go. Who knows what challenge is next for you? Just be careful out there, Master of Adventure!

GRAND TALLY

So how did you do? Are you king of the animal kingdom? Earth explorer extraordinaire? Prince or princess of pop culture? Wonder woman of the wilderness? Magnificent mad scientist? Tally your scores from all eight chapters to learn how you stack up against other brainiacs. Use the chart below to find your *Quiz Whiz* status.

0–330

TRIVIA TRAINEE
You have only begun to dabble in details. With a score like this, you may think you need to hit the books. However, your healthy curiosity about how the world works makes you an interesting companion! Play detective and keep asking questions to flex that brain muscle. Knowledge is power!

331–625

SEMI-PRO PLAYER
As far as facts go, you're on the ball! You are a qualified Quiz Whiz! To become a more well-rounded quizmeister, tap into your curiosity about topics you haven't much experience with. You may just find a new passion!

626–1,000

MASTER FACT BLASTER
Your encyclopedic knowledge can't be topped. You are a wizard of words, a superstar speaker of sensational facts, a victor of verifiable info. Congratulations on a job well done!

46, (tl) Eric IsselÄe/Shutterstock; 46, (br) Benedictus/Shutterstock; 47, (bc) Jeff Kinsey/ Shutterstock; 47, (tr) Pavel Cheiko/Shutterstock; 47, (cl) Jenny Solomon/iStockphoto; 48, (c) Philip Game/Getty Images; 48, (bl) Accent Alaska/Alamy; 48, (bc) Frans Lanting/ National Geographic Stock; 48, (br) Stephen Frink/Getty Images; 49, (tr) Quinn Rooney/ Getty Images; 49, (tc) David Keaton/Corbis; 49, (bc) Tui De Roy/Getty Images; 50, (game show host illustration) Dan Sipple; 50, (cr) Yasonya/Shutterstock; 50, (bc) Rich Carey/ Shutterstock; 51, (bl) Espen E/Shutterstock; 51, (br) Deejpilot/iStockphoto; 51, (tcl) stocker1970/Shutterstock; 51, (cl) Nickolay Vinokurov/Shutterstock; 51, (cr) ben bryant/ Shutterstock; 51, (tr) gagliardifoto/Shutterstock; 51, (bc) Vladitto/Shutterstock; 51, (bcr) Mark Schwettmann/Shutterstock

Pop Culture [52-65]
52-53, (Main) DreamWorks/Courtesy Everett Collection; 54, (tl) Charley Gallay/WireImage/ Gettyimages; 54, (r) Archives du 7e; 54, (bl) Randy Miramontez/Shutterstock; 55, (t) Joe Seer/Shutterstock ; 56, (bl) Blulz60/Shutterstock; 56, (cr) Archives du 7eme Art/Archives du 7e; 56, (tl) RamonaS/Shutterstock; 57, (br) E. Dougherty/WireImage/Getty Images; 57, (cl) Pushkin/Shutterstock; 60, (tl) carrie-nelson/Shutterstock; 60, (cr) Brad Camembert/ Shutterstock; 60, (bl) Ververidis Vasilis/Shutterstock; 61, (c) Featureflash/Shutterstock; 62-63, (bkgd) age fotostock/SuperStock; 64, (game show host illustration) Dan Sipple; 64, (tr) Paul Erickson/iStockphoto; 64, (c) Aleksey Stemmer/Shutterstock; 65, (br) Archives du 7e Art/Dreamworks/Archives du 7e; 65, (r) rook76/Shutterstock; 65, (cr) Helga Esteb/ Shutterstock; 65, (tcr) s_bukley/Shutterstock; 65, (cl) s_bukley/Shutterstock; 65, (tcl) Debby Wong/Shutterstock; 65, (bcl) Mim Friday/Alamy; 65, (bcr) Archives du 7e; 65, (bl) AF archive/Alamy; 65, (br) Shaun Kemper/Alamy.

Get Back to Nature [66-83]
66-67, (Main) John Shaw/Photo Researchers/Getty Images; 68-69, (Main) Alexander Ishchenko/Shutterstock; 70, (cl) Viktor1/Shutterstock.com; 70-71, (bc) Diana Taliun/ Shutterstock; 71, (tr) Denise Kappa/Shutterstock; 71, (cr) Suede Chen/Shutterstock; 71, (br) stocksolutions/Shutterstock; 72-73, (Main) Jamen Percy/Shutterstock; 74, (tc) Nataliya Hora/Shutterstock; 74, (bl) Ladislav Pavliha/E+/Getty Images; 74, (bc) Mac99/iStockphoto; 74, (br) Paul Orr/Shutterstock; 75, (br) Minerva Studio/Shutterstock; 75, (tc) Mike Theiss/ National Geographic/Getty Images; 76, (tl) Dmytro Pylypenko/Alamy; 76, (cr) Dan Leeth/ Alamy; 76, (bl) imagebroker.net/SuperStock ; 77, (r) Jan Martin Will/Shutterstock; 77, (cl) Pan Xunbin/Shutterstock; 80-81, (Main) mikenorton/Shutterstock; 82, (game show host illustration) Dan Sipple; 82, (tr) Tobik/Shutterstock; 82, (bl) NOAA via Getty Images; 83, (tcl) Ryan M. Bolton/Shutterstock; 83, (tl) reptiles4all/Shutterstock; 83, (tr) Mircea BEZERGHEANU/Shutterstock; 83, (tcr) Debbie Lund/iStockphoto; 83, (br) WILLIAM WEST/ AFP/Getty Images

Blast from the Past [84-105]
84-85, (Main) Algol/Shutterstock; 86, (tl) Wessam Eldeeb /iStockphoto; 86, (cr) Vertes Edmond Mihai/Shutterstock; 86, (bl) Lachlan Currie/iStockphoto; 87, (tr) William Thomas Cain/Getty Images News/Getty Images; 87, (cl) Blulz60/Shutterstock; 87, (bc) MCT/ McClatchy-Tribune/Getty Images; 88-89, (bkgd) Anastasija Popova/Shutterstock; 90, (cr) Michael Ochs Archives/Getty Images; 90, (cl) Chip Somodevilla/Getty Images; 90, (br) iofoto/

Shutterstock; 90, (tl) Evening Standard/Hulton Archive/Getty Images; 91, (tr) George De Sota/Redferns/Getty Images; 91, (cl) PHOTO MEDIA/ClassicStock/Corbis; 91, (br) Michael Ochs Archives/Getty Images; 92, (bl) Sergey Uryadnikov/Shutterstock; 92, (cr) Ariel Bravy/Shutterstock; 92, (tl) BioLife Pics/Shutterstock; 92-93, (b) Elena Elisseeva/Shutersock; 93, (tr) Pierdelune/Shutterstock; 93, (bl) Steve Bower/Shutterstock; 94-95, (bkgd) debr22pics/Shutterstock; 96-97, (bkgd) Mariusz S. Jurgielewicz/Shutterstock; 98, (tr) Ben Molyneux/Alamy; 98, (cl) AF archive/Alamy; 98, (br) Archives du 7e; 99, (bl) Urbano Delvalle/Time & Life Pictures/Getty Images; 99, (tr) Fred de Noyelle/Godong/Corbis; 100-101, (bkgd) Pichugin Dmitry /Shutterstock; 102, (br) Jane Rix/Shutterstock; 102, (bl) Cameron Davidson/Corbis; 102, (tc) Michael S. Yamashita/CORBIS; 103, (bc) Jan Woitas/dpa/Corbis; 103, (tc) North Wind Picture Archives/Alamy; 103, (br) Scott Olson/Getty Images News/Getty Images; 104, (game show host illustration) Dan Sipple; 104, (tr) Olivier/Shutterstock; 104, (cl) Videowokart/Shutterstock; 104, (cr) Michael S. Yamashita/CORBIS; 104, (bcl) Dreamworks Animation/The Kobal Collection/Art Resource; 105, (bc) Denys Kurbatov/Shutterstock; 105, (br) Keystone-France/Gamma-Keystone/Getty Images; 105, (tcl) CBS Photo Archive/CBS/Getty Images; 105, (tcr) MGM Studios/Moviepix/Getty Images; 105, (bcl) Michael Ochs Archives/Moviepix/Getty Images; 105, (bcr) AF archive/Alamy

It All Adds Up [106-121]
106-107, (bkgd) Dhoxax/Shutterstock; 108, (cl) gillmar/Shutterstock; 108, (br) Shawn Hempel/Shutterstock; 109, (tr) Zuzule/Shutterstock; 109, (cl) Africa Studio/Shutterstock; 109, (br) Africa Studio/Shutterstock; 110-111, (bkgd) fortuna777/Shutterstock; 112, (tl) 18percentgrey/Shutterstock; 112, (cr) nui7711/Shutterstock; 112, (bl) HixnHix/Shutterstock; 113, (l) Dario sabljak/Shutterstock; 113, (cr) MillaF/Shutterstock; 116-117, (bkgd) Dioscoro L. Dioticio/Shutterstock; 116-117, (bkgd) Daniel Tang/iStockphoto; 118, (c) PHB.cz (Richard Semik)/Shutterstock; 118, (bl) Neale Cousland/Shutterstock; 118, (cr) little photographer/Shutterstock; 119, (tr) LaurensT/Shutterstock; 119, (cr) Jelle vd Wolf/Shutterstock; 119, (bl) cesc_assawin/Shutterstock; 120, (game show host illustration) Dan Sipple; 120, (tr) Ian Rentoul/Shutterstock; 120, (cr) Goncharuk/Shutterstock; 120, (bc) Nikola Bilic/iStockphoto; 121, (bl) Michael Durham/Minden Pictures/Getty Images; 121, (bcl) Arsgera/Shutterstock; 121, (bcr) Heiko Kiera/Shutterstock; 121, (br) Sari ONeal/Shutterstock; 121, (tcl) Four Oaks/Shutterstock; 121, (tcr) Alexia Khruscheva/Shutterstock; 121, (cl) noolwlee/Shutterstock; 121, (RT CTR) StHelena/iStockphoto

Weird Science [122-141]
122-123, (bkgd) Andrew Rich/iStockphoto; 124-125, (Main) Yuri Arcurs/Shutterstock; 126, (tcr) A. FILIS/AP Images; 126, (cl) Gerald & Buff Corsi/Visuals Unlimited/Corbis; 126, (bl) Wim van Egmond/Visuals Unlimited/Corbis; 127, (tl) totophotos/Shutterstock; 127, (cr) blickwinkel/Alamy; 127, (cl) SAM YEH/AFP/Getty Images; 127, (br) Dante Fenolio/Photo Researchers/Getty Images; 128-129, (bkgd) BSG Designer; 130, (cl) Mitsuhiko Imamori/Minden Pictures/Corbis; 130, (br) alslutsky/Shutterstock; 130, (tr) Dani Vincek/Shutterstock; 131, (tr) Moviestore collection Ltd/Alamy; 131, (br) Claudio Divizia/Shutterstock; 134-135, (bkgd) Max Sudakov/Shutterstock; 136-137, (bc) y&s creators/Alamy; 136, (tr) Ariel Bravy/Shutterstock; 136, (bl) DAN SUZIO/Photo Researchers/Getty Images; 137, (tl) zyxeos30/iStockphoto; 137, (cr) Eugene Sergeev/Shutterstock; 138, (cr) Samadelli Marco/EURAC/dpa/Corbis; 138, (bl) Michael Nicholson/Corbis; 138, (bc) HO/

Reuters/Corbis; 138, (br) Kumar Sriskandan/Alamy; 139, (tc) Mark Wilson/Getty Images; 139, (br) Francis Latreille; 140, (game show host illustration) Dan Sipple; 140, (cr) Martin Froyda/Shutterstock; 140, (br) Ingo Arndt/Minden Pictures/Getty Images; 140, (bl) Cosmin Manci/Shutterstock; 141, (tl)/Time & Life Pictures/Getty Images; 141, (tr) Frank Greenaway/Getty Images; 141, (c) Stocktrek/Getty Images; 141, (bl) Reinhard Dirscherl/Getty Images; 141, (bcl) AFP/Getty Images; 141, (bcr) Marco Prosch/Getty Images; 141, (br) Imaginechina/Corbis

Global Adventures [142-157]
142-143, (Main) Makushin Alexey/Shutterstock; 144, (cr) Adam Dodd/iStockphoto; 144, (tr) Ailani Graphics/Shutterstock; 144, (bl) Roll Call/Getty Images; 144, (LE CTR) zorpink/Shutterstock; 145, (br) Jeff Whyte/Shutterstock; 145, (tl) Time & Life Pictures/Getty Images ; 146-147, (bkgd) ZUMA Press, Inc./Alamy; 150-151, (bkgd) Ryan Pyle/Corbis; 150-151, Uschools University Images/iStockphoto; 152, (tl) Peter Dean/Alamy; 152-153, (br) mitchellpictures/iStockphoto; 153, (cl) Hung Chung Chih/Shutterstock; 153, (br) Antonio Petrone/Shutterstock; 154, (bl) Chris A Crumley/Alamy; 154, (c) Brian Cahn/ZUMA Press/Corbis; 154, (br) GARY BOGDON KRT/Newscom; 155, (tc) Bob Thomas/Popperfoto/Getty Images; 155, (br) Adam Eastland Italy/Alamy; 155, (bl) TAO Images Limited/Getty Images; 156, (game show host illustration) Dan Sipple; 156, (br) Lebrecht Music and Arts Photo Library/Alamy; 156, (tcl) WPA Pool/Getty Images News/Getty Images; 156, (UPRT-B) Matt84/iStockphoto; 156, (cl) Bettmann/CORBIS; 156, (cr) Georgios Kollidas/Shutterstock; 156, (bl) Anchorage Daily News/McClatchy-Tribune/Getty Images; 157, (tl) Atlaspix/Shutterstock; 157, (br) Tom Briglia/FilmMagic/Getty Images

Answer Key [158-170]
158, (tc) efendy/Shutterstock; 158, (bcl) wong yu liang/Shutterstock; 158, (tr) Denis Vesely/Shutterstock; 159, (tr) Leo Shoot/Shutterstock; 159, (bc) Worakit Sirijinda/Shutterstock; 160, (tr) Eric IsselÄe/Shutterstock; 160, (c) Cgissemann/Shutterstock; 160, (br) Stuart Westmorland/Getty Images; 160, (bc) Accent Alaska/Alamy; 161, (c) Joe Seer/Shutterstock; 162, (c) Paul Erickson/iStockphoto; 162, (cr) Archives du 7e Art/Dreamworks/Photos 12/Alamy; 163, (tc) Minerva Studio/Shutterstock; 163, (cl) Denise Kappa/Shutterstock; 163, (c) Jan Martin Will/Shutterstock; 164, (tc) Debbie Lund/iStockphoto; 164, (bl) Vertes Edmond Mihai/Shutterstock; 164, (br) Michael Ochs Archives/Getty Images; 165, (cr) AF archive/Alamy; 166, (tl) gillmar/Shutterstock; 166, (cr) LaurensT/Shutterstock; 166, (br) Darrin Henry/iStockphoto; 167, (bl) Yuri Arcurs/Shutterstock; 167, (c) Dani Vincek/Shutterstock; 168, (c) DAN SUZIO/Photo Researchers/Getty Images; 168, (tr) Eugene Sergeev/Shutterstock; 168, (cr) Mark Wilson/Getty Images; 169, (cl) Jeff Whyte/Shutterstock; 169, (tc) Daniel Mitchell/iStockphoto; 169, (cr) Brian Cahn/ZUMA Press/Corbis; 169, (br) Tom Briglia/FilmMagic/Getty Images; 170, (bl) Igor Kovalchuk/Shutterstock; 170, (bc) Brian Tan/Shutterstock; 170, (br) Ivonne Wierink/Shutterstock; 175, oorka/Shutterstock; 175, Petr84/Shutterstock

**Published by the
National Geographic Society**
John M. Fahey, Jr., *Chairman of the Board and
Chief Executive Officer*
Declan Moore, *Executive Vice President;
President, Publishing and Travel*
Melina Gerosa Bellows, *Executive Vice
President; Chief Creative Officer, Books,
Kids, and Family*

Prepared by the Book Division
Hector Sierra, *Senior Vice President
and General Manager*
Nancy Laties Feresten, *Senior Vice President, Kids
Publishing and Media*
Jay Sumner, *Director of Photography,
Children's Publishing*
Jennifer Emmett, *Vice President,
Editorial Director, Children's Books*
Eva Absher-Schantz, *Design Director, Kids
Publishing and Media*
R. Gary Colbert, *Production Director*
Jennifer A. Thornton, *Director of Managing
Editorial*

Staff for This Book
Robin Terry, *Project Editor*
Eva Absher-Schantz, *Art Director*
Kelley Miller, *Senior Illustrations Editor*
Sven M. Dolling, *Map Research and Production*
Grace Hill, *Associate Managing Editor*
Joan Gossett, *Production Editor*
Lewis R. Bassford, *Production Manager*
Callie Broaddus, *Design Production Assistant*
Susan Borke, *Legal and Business Affairs*

**Editorial, Design and Production by
Q2A/Bill Smith**

Production Services
Phillip L. Schlosser, *Senior Vice President*
Chris Brown, *Vice President, NG Book
Manufacturing*
George Bounelis, *Vice President, Production
Services*
Nicole Elliott, *Manager*
Rachel Faulise, *Manager*
Robert L. Barr, *Manager*

The National Geographic Society is
one of the world's largest non-
profit scientific and educational
organizations. Founded in 1888
to "increase and diffuse geographic knowledge," the Society
works to inspire people to care
about the planet. National Geographic reflects
the world through its magazines, television
programs, films, music and radio, books, DVDs,
maps, exhibitions, live events, school publishing programs, interactive media and mer-
chandise. *National Geographic* magazine, the
Society's official journal, published in English
and 38 local-language editions, is read by more
than 60 million people each month. The National Geographic Channel reaches 440 million
households in 38 languages in 171 countries.
National Geographic Digital Media receives
more than 25 million visitors a month. National
Geographic has funded more than 10,000 scientific research, conservation and exploration
projects and supports an education program
promoting geography literacy.

For more information, please visit
nationalgeographic.com, call
1-800-NGS LINE (647-5463), or write
to the following address:
National Geographic Society
1145 17th Street N.W.
Washington, D.C. 20036-4688 U.S.A.

Visit us online at
nationalgeographic.com/books

For librarians and teachers:
ngchildrensbooks.org

More for kids from National Geographic:
kids.nationalgeographic.com

For information about special discounts
for bulk purchases, please contact
National Geographic Books Special Sales:
ngspecsales@ngs.org

For rights or permissions inquiries, please
contact National Geographic Books Subsidiary
Rights: ngbookrights@ngs.org

Paperback ISBN: 978-1-4263-1356-1
Library ISBN: 978-1-4263-1357-8

Printed in U.S.A.
13/QGT-CML/1